NEWARK PUBLIC LIBRARY

BREATH OF BONES™

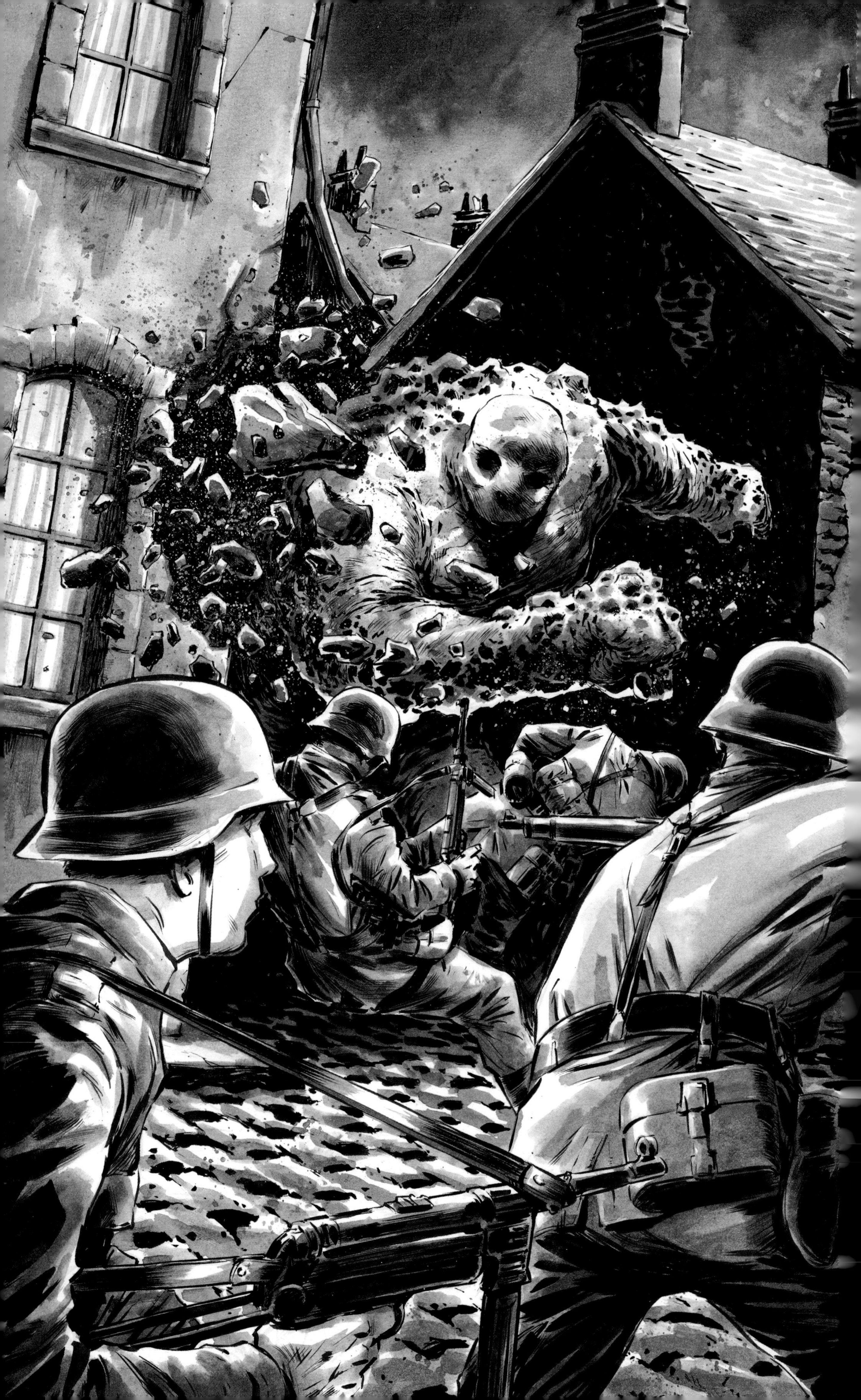

BREATH OF BONES

A TALE OF THE GOLEM

Story
STEVE NILES and MATT SANTORO

Script
STEVE NILES

Art
DAVE WACHTER

Letters
NATE PIEKOS of BLAMBOT®

DARK HORSE BOOKS

Assistant Editor
SHANTEL LaROCQUE

Designer
AMY ARENDTS

Neil Hankerson *Executive Vice President* · Tom Weddle *Chief Financial Officer* · Randy Stradley *Vice President of Publishing* Michael Martens *Vice President of Book Trade Sales* · Anita Nelson *Vice President of Business Affairs* · Scott Allie *Editor in Chief* Matt Parkinson *Vice President of Marketing* · David Scroggy *Vice President of Product Development* · Dale LaFountain *Vice President of Information Technology* · Darlene Vogel *Senior Director of Print, Design, and Production* · Ken Lizzi *General Counsel* Davey Estrada *Editorial Director* · Chris Warner *Senior Books Editor* · Diana Schutz *Executive Editor* · Cary Grazzini *Director of Print and Development* · Lia Ribacchi *Art Director* · Cara Niece *Director of Scheduling* · Tim Wiesch *Director of International Licensing* · Mark Bernardi *Director of Digital Publishing*

BREATH OF BONES: A TALE OF THE GOLEM

© 2013, 2014 Steve Niles, Matt Santoro, and Dave Wachter. Breath of Bones™ and all prominently featured characters are trademarks of Steve Niles, Matt Santoro, and Dave Wachter. Dark Horse Books® and the Dark Horse logo are registered trademarks of Dark Horse Comics, Inc. All rights reserved. No portion of this publication may be reproduced or transmitted, in any form or by any means, without the express written permission of Dark Horse Comics, Inc. Names, characters, places, and incidents featured in this publication either are the product of the author's imagination or are used fictitiously. Any resemblance to actual persons (living or dead), events, institutions, or locales, without satiric intent, is coincidental.

This volume reprints the comic-book series *Breath of Bones: A Tale of the Golem* #1–#3 from Dark Horse Comics.

Published by Dark Horse Books
A division of Dark Horse Comics, Inc.
10956 SE Main Street
Milwaukie, OR 97222

DarkHorse.com

International Licensing: (503) 905-2377

To find a comics shop in your area, call the Comic Shop Locator Service toll-free at (888) 266-4226.

First edition: February 2014
ISBN 978-1-61655-344-9

10 9 8 7 6 5 4 3 2
Printed in China

CHAPTER ONE

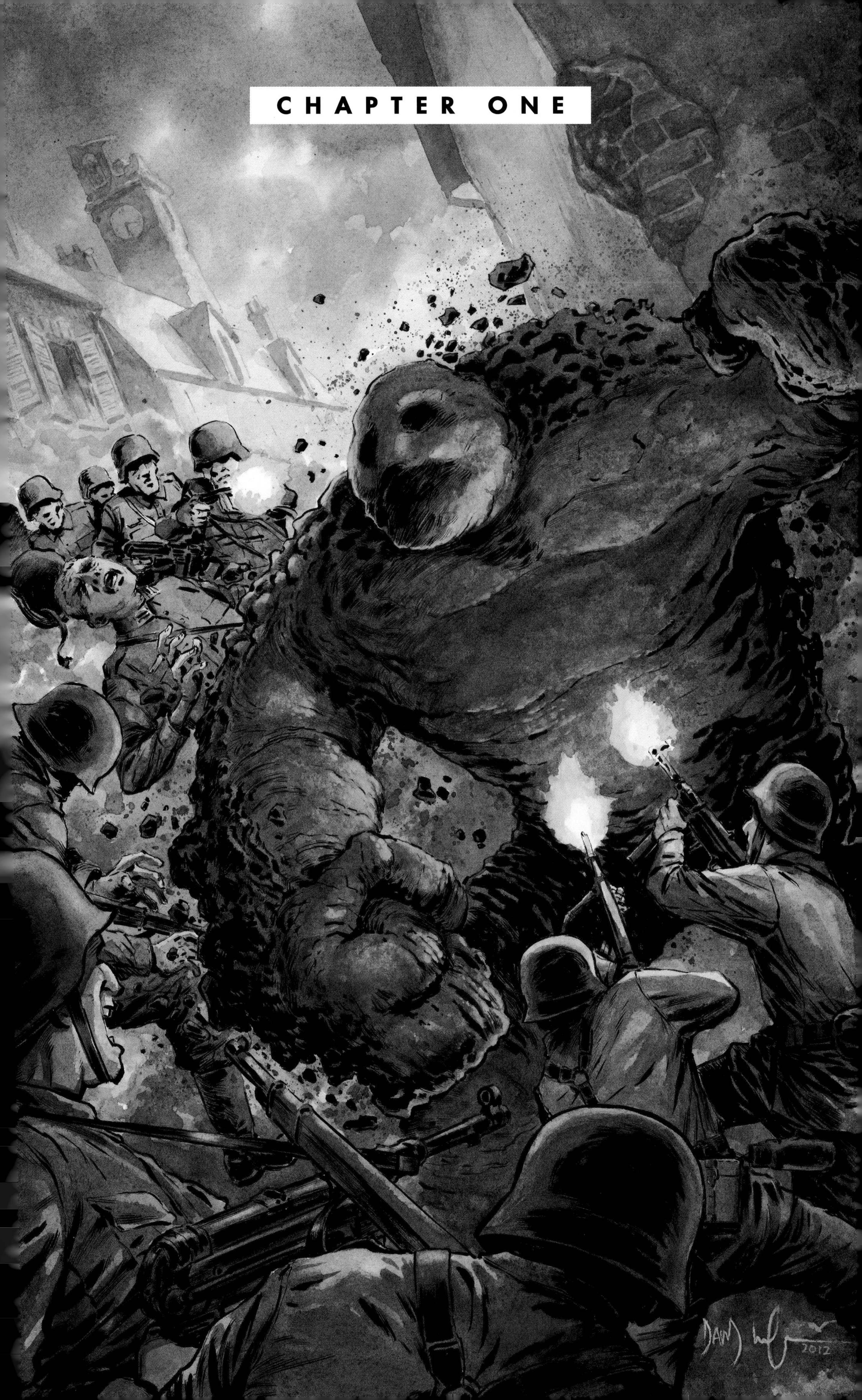

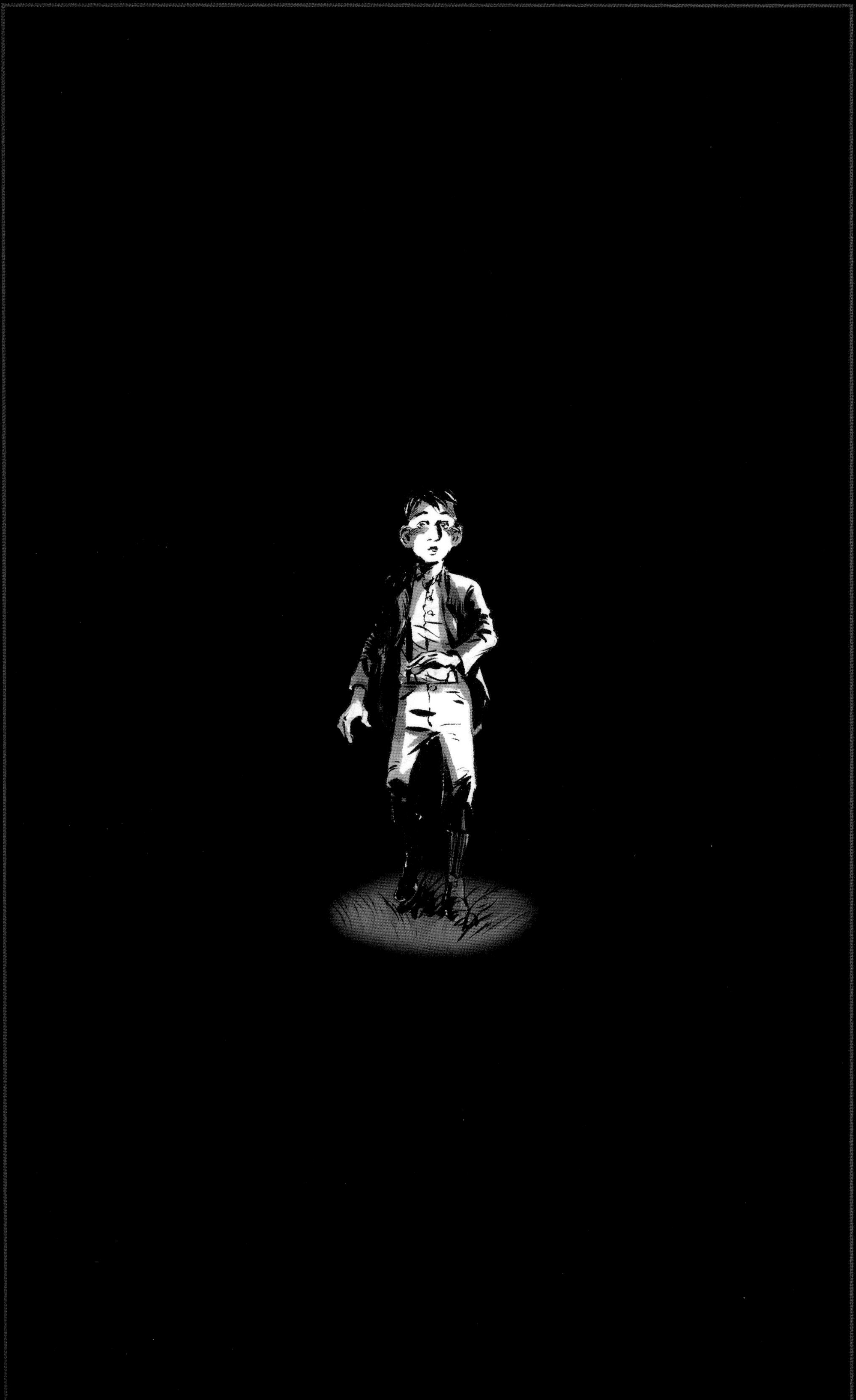

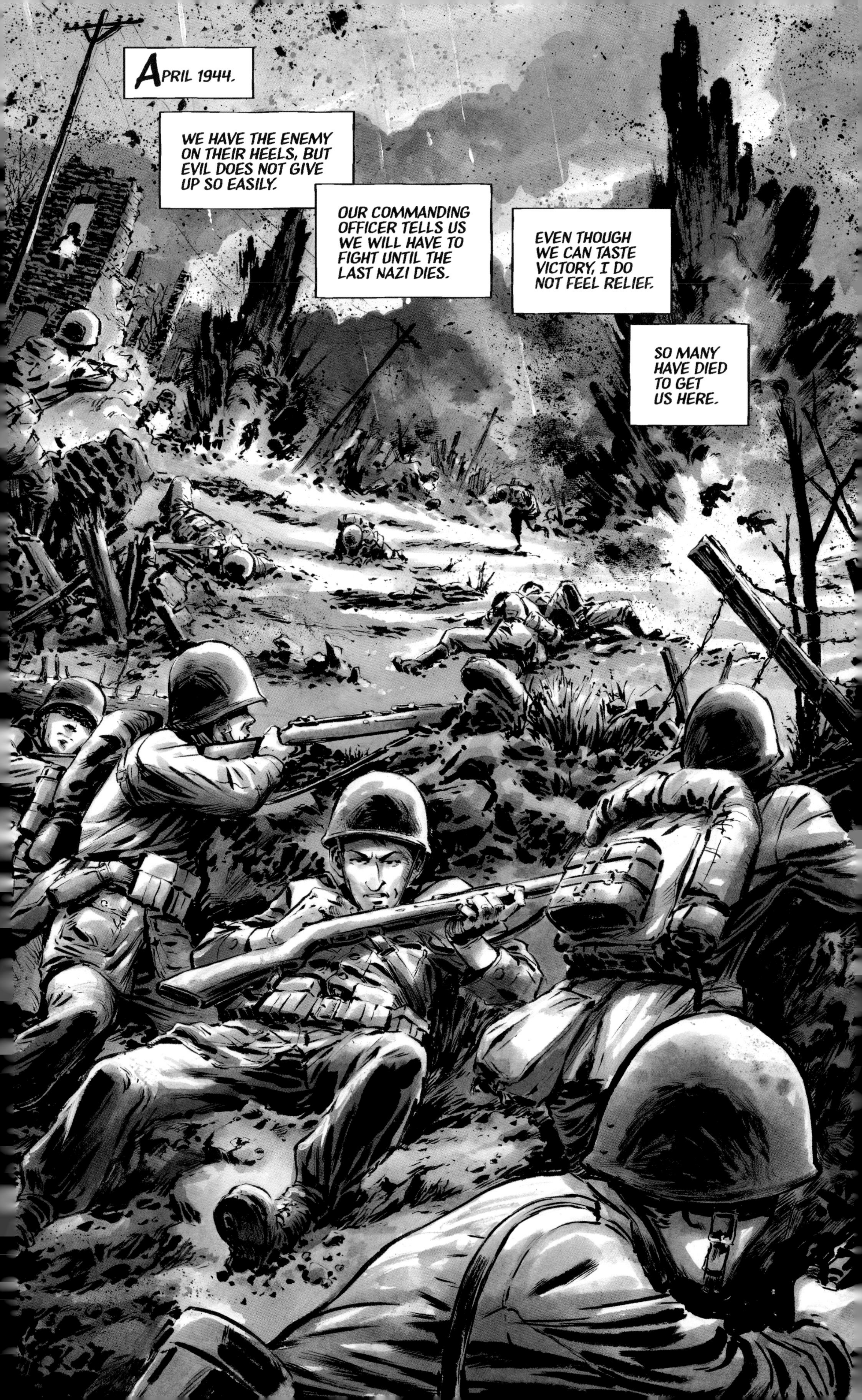
APRIL 1944.
WE HAVE THE ENEMY ON THEIR HEELS, BUT EVIL DOES NOT GIVE UP SO EASILY.
OUR COMMANDING OFFICER TELLS US WE WILL HAVE TO FIGHT UNTIL THE LAST NAZI DIES.
EVEN THOUGH WE CAN TASTE VICTORY, I DO NOT FEEL RELIEF.
SO MANY HAVE DIED TO GET US HERE.

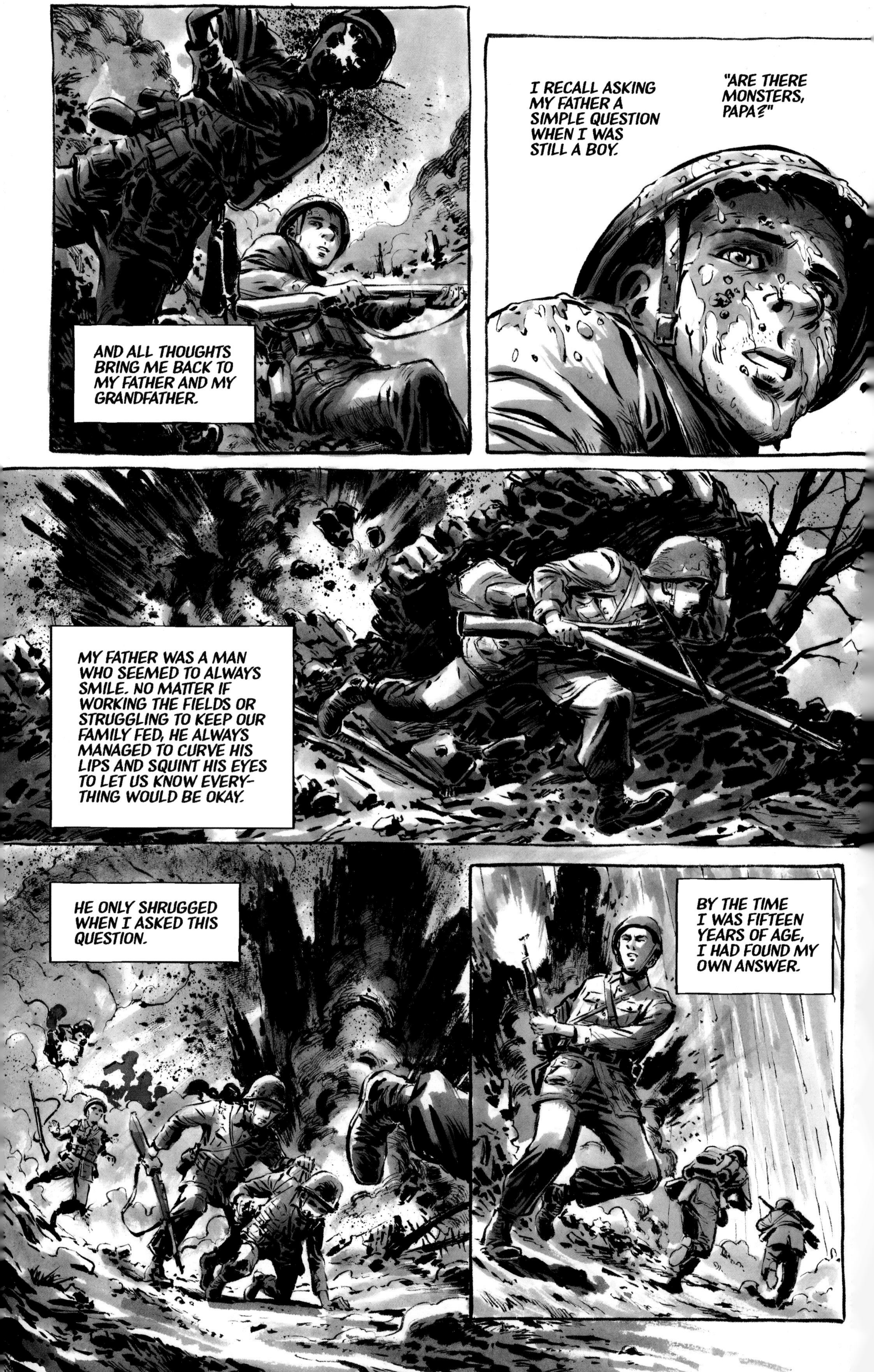
AND ALL THOUGHTS BRING ME BACK TO MY FATHER AND MY GRANDFATHER.
I RECALL ASKING MY FATHER A SIMPLE QUESTION WHEN I WAS STILL A BOY.
"ARE THERE MONSTERS, PAPA?"
MY FATHER WAS A MAN WHO SEEMED TO ALWAYS SMILE. NO MATTER IF WORKING THE FIELDS OR STRUGGLING TO KEEP OUR FAMILY FED, HE ALWAYS MANAGED TO CURVE HIS LIPS AND SQUINT HIS EYES TO LET US KNOW EVERY-THING WOULD BE OKAY.
HE ONLY SHRUGGED WHEN I ASKED THIS QUESTION.
BY THE TIME I WAS FIFTEEN YEARS OF AGE, I HAD FOUND MY OWN ANSWER.

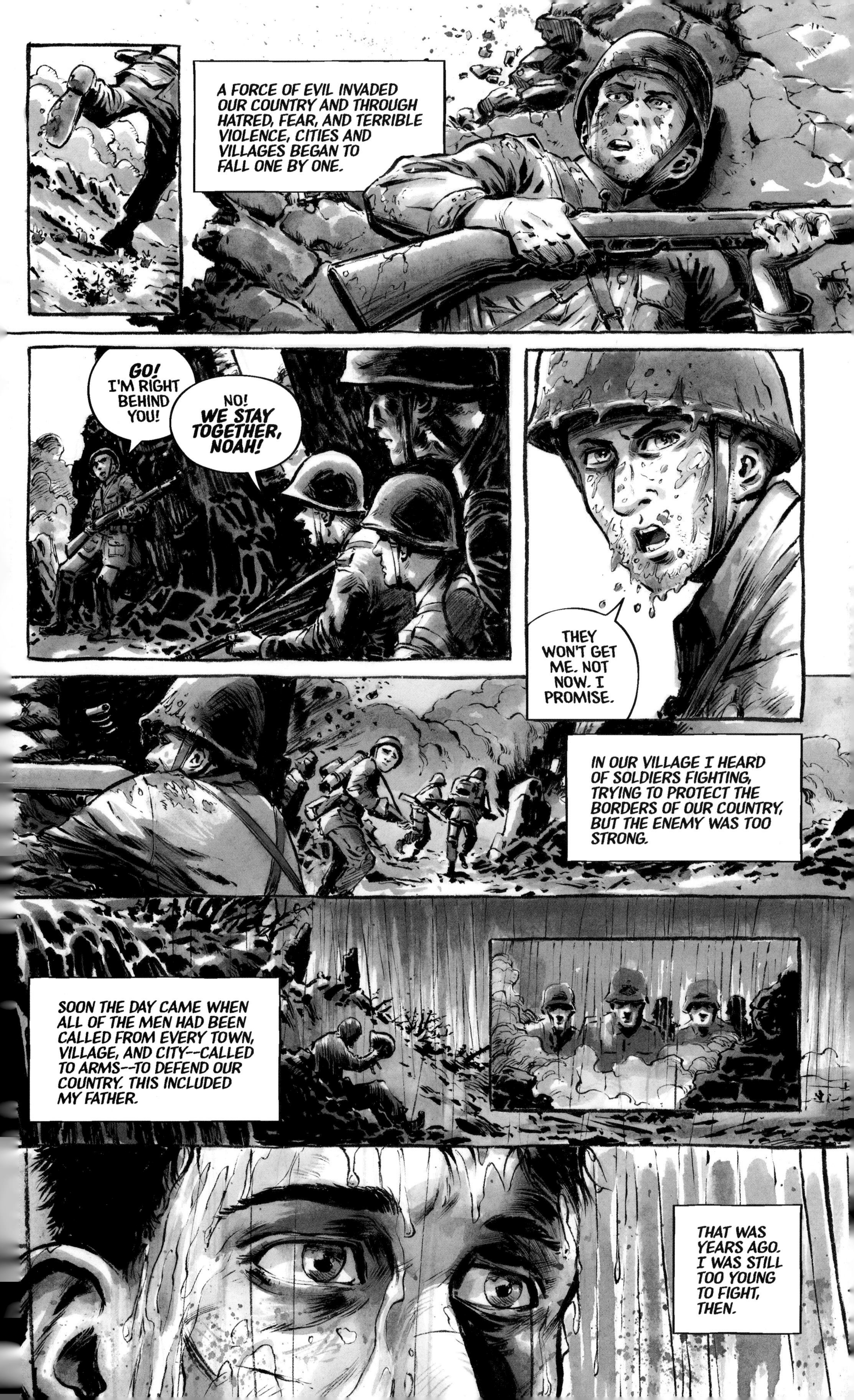
A FORCE OF EVIL INVADED OUR COUNTRY AND THROUGH HATRED, FEAR, AND TERRIBLE VIOLENCE, CITIES AND VILLAGES BEGAN TO FALL ONE BY ONE.
GO! I'M RIGHT BEHIND YOU!
NO! WE STAY TOGETHER, NOAH!
THEY WON'T GET ME. NOT NOW. I PROMISE.
IN OUR VILLAGE I HEARD OF SOLDIERS FIGHTING, TRYING TO PROTECT THE BORDERS OF OUR COUNTRY, BUT THE ENEMY WAS TOO STRONG.
SOON THE DAY CAME WHEN ALL OF THE MEN HAD BEEN CALLED FROM EVERY TOWN, VILLAGE, AND CITY--CALLED TO ARMS--TO DEFEND OUR COUNTRY. THIS INCLUDED MY FATHER.
THAT WAS YEARS AGO. I WAS STILL TOO YOUNG TO FIGHT, THEN.

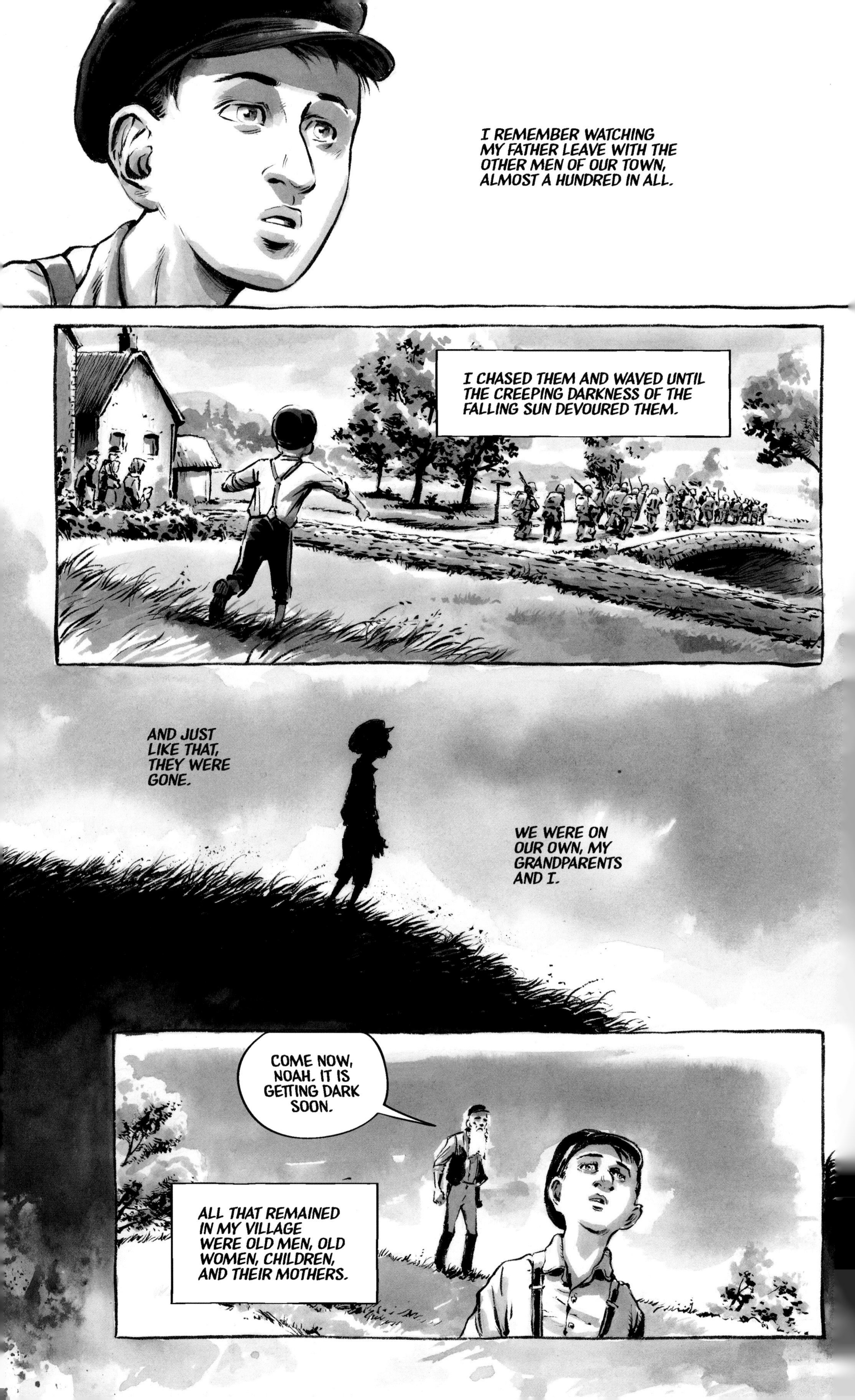
I REMEMBER WATCHING MY FATHER LEAVE WITH THE OTHER MEN OF OUR TOWN, ALMOST A HUNDRED IN ALL.
I CHASED THEM AND WAVED UNTIL THE CREEPING DARKNESS OF THE FALLING SUN DEVOURED THEM.
AND JUST LIKE THAT, THEY WERE GONE.
WE WERE ON OUR OWN, MY GRANDPARENTS AND I.
COME NOW, NOAH. IT IS GETTING DARK SOON.
ALL THAT REMAINED IN MY VILLAGE WERE OLD MEN, OLD WOMEN, CHILDREN, AND THEIR MOTHERS.

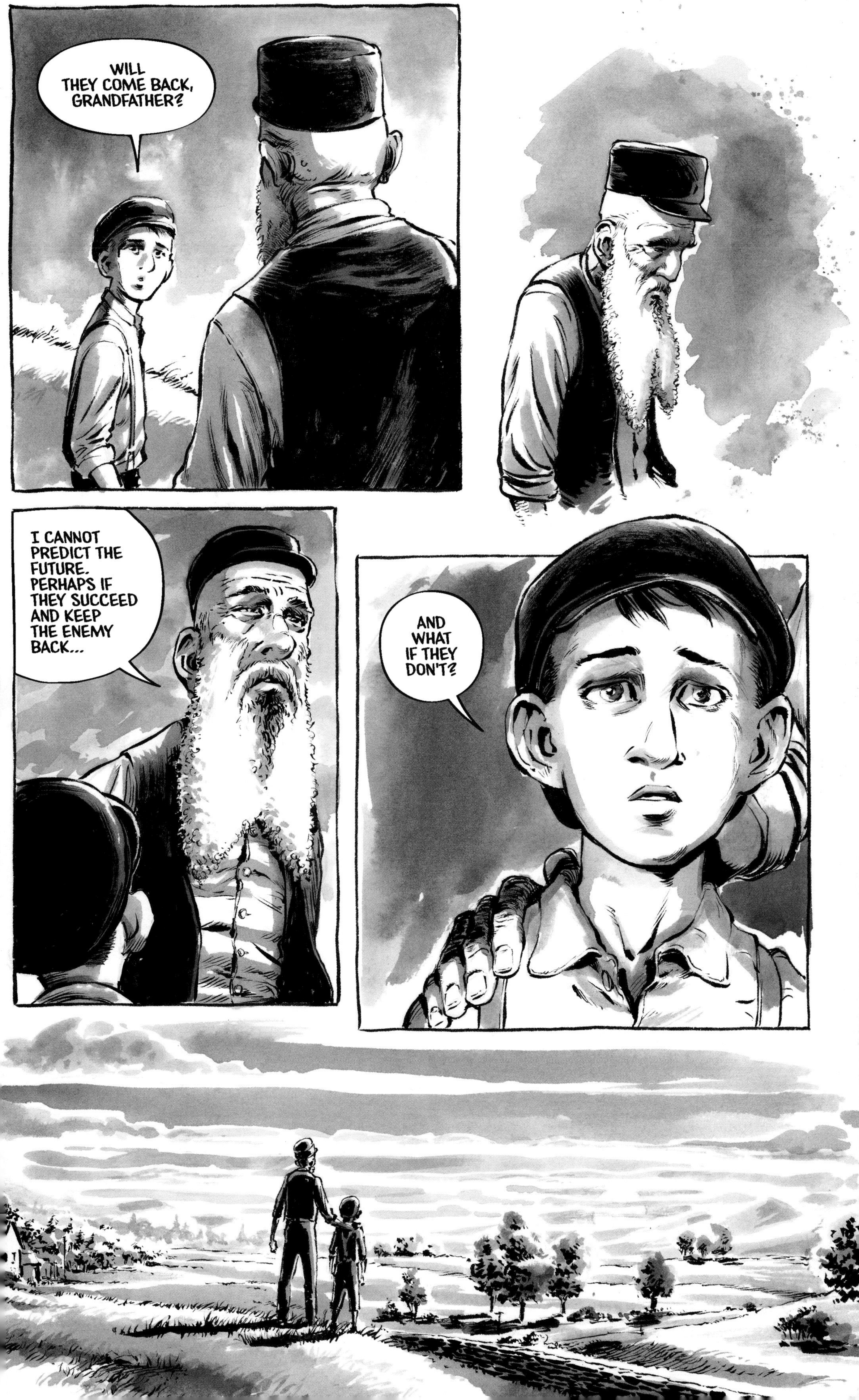
WILL THEY COME BACK, GRANDFATHER?
I CANNOT PREDICT THE FUTURE. PERHAPS IF THEY SUCCEED AND KEEP THE ENEMY BACK...
AND WHAT IF THEY DON'T?

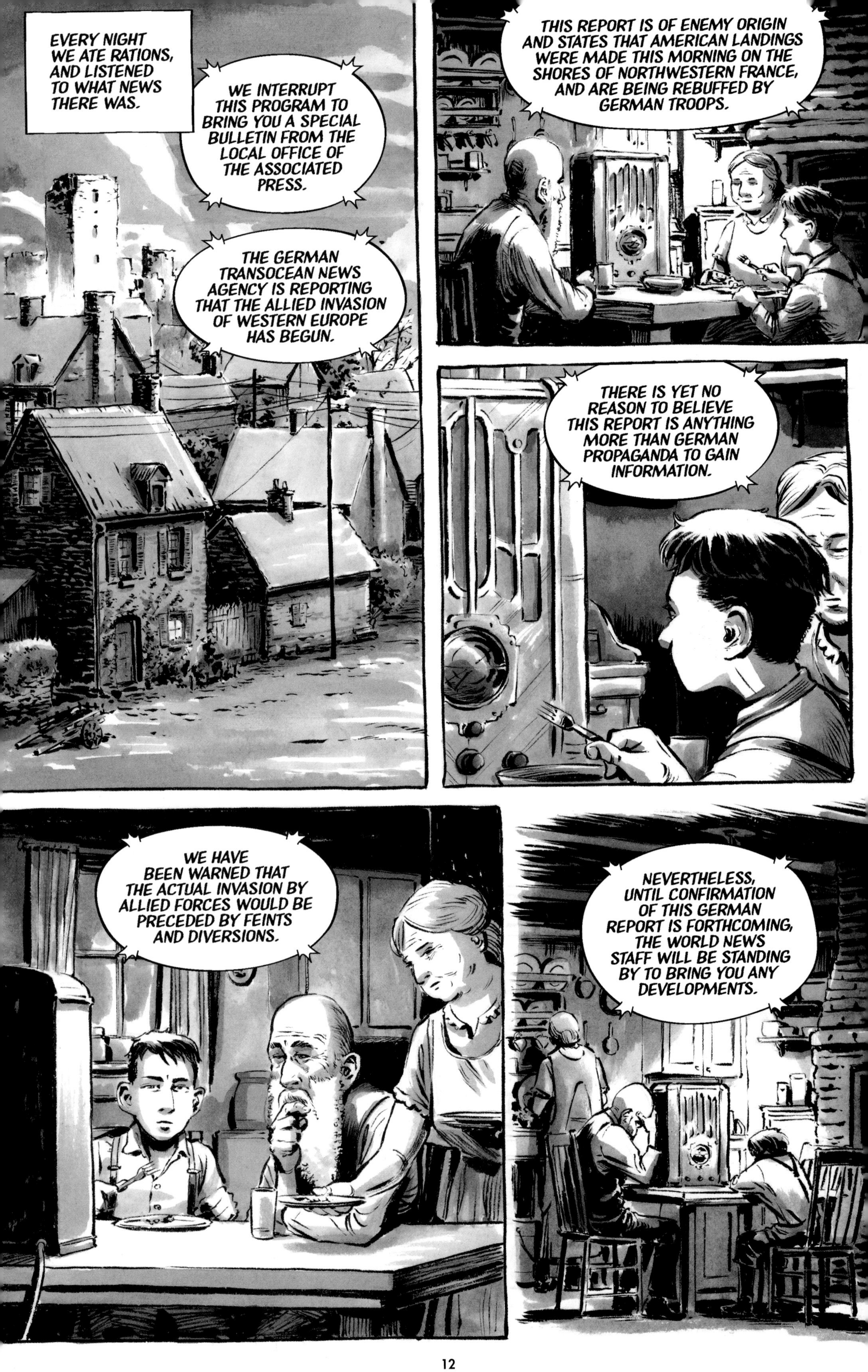
EVERY NIGHT WE ATE RATIONS, AND LISTENED TO WHAT NEWS THERE WAS.
WE INTERRUPT THIS PROGRAM TO BRING YOU A SPECIAL BULLETIN FROM THE LOCAL OFFICE OF THE ASSOCIATED PRESS.
THE GERMAN TRANSOCEAN NEWS AGENCY IS REPORTING THAT THE ALLIED INVASION OF WESTERN EUROPE HAS BEGUN.
THIS REPORT IS OF ENEMY ORIGIN AND STATES THAT AMERICAN LANDINGS WERE MADE THIS MORNING ON THE SHORES OF NORTHWESTERN FRANCE, AND ARE BEING REBUFFED BY GERMAN TROOPS.
THERE IS YET NO REASON TO BELIEVE THIS REPORT IS ANYTHING MORE THAN GERMAN PROPAGANDA TO GAIN INFORMATION.
WE HAVE BEEN WARNED THAT THE ACTUAL INVASION BY ALLIED FORCES WOULD BE PRECEDED BY FEINTS AND DIVERSIONS.
NEVERTHELESS, UNTIL CONFIRMATION OF THIS GERMAN REPORT IS FORTHCOMING, THE WORLD NEWS STAFF WILL BE STANDING BY TO BRING YOU ANY DEVELOPMENTS.

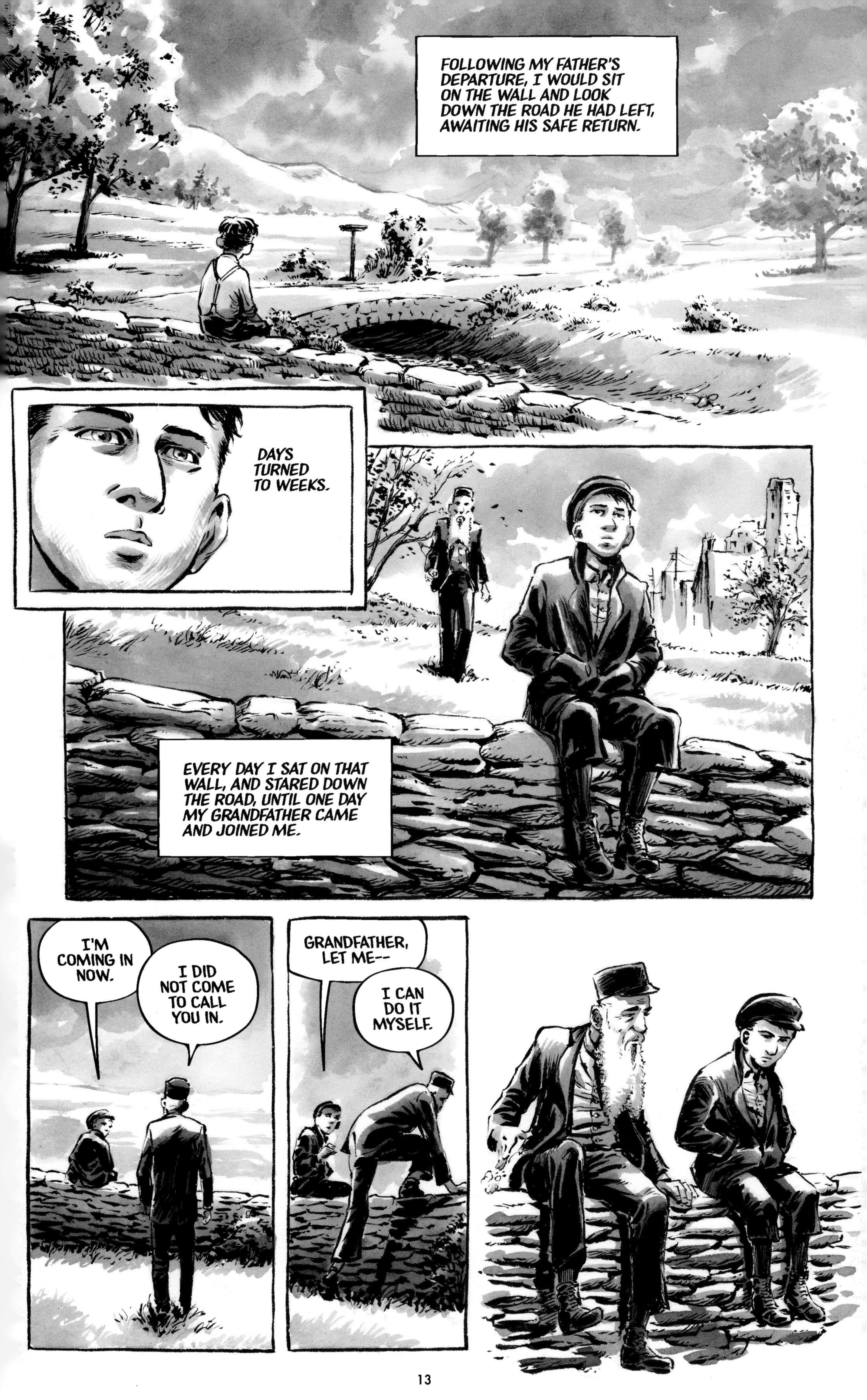
FOLLOWING MY FATHER'S DEPARTURE, I WOULD SIT ON THE WALL AND LOOK DOWN THE ROAD HE HAD LEFT, AWAITING HIS SAFE RETURN.
DAYS TURNED TO WEEKS.
EVERY DAY I SAT ON THAT WALL, AND STARED DOWN THE ROAD, UNTIL ONE DAY MY GRANDFATHER CAME AND JOINED ME.
I'M COMING IN NOW.
I DID NOT COME TO CALL YOU IN.
GRANDFATHER, LET ME--
I CAN DO IT MYSELF.

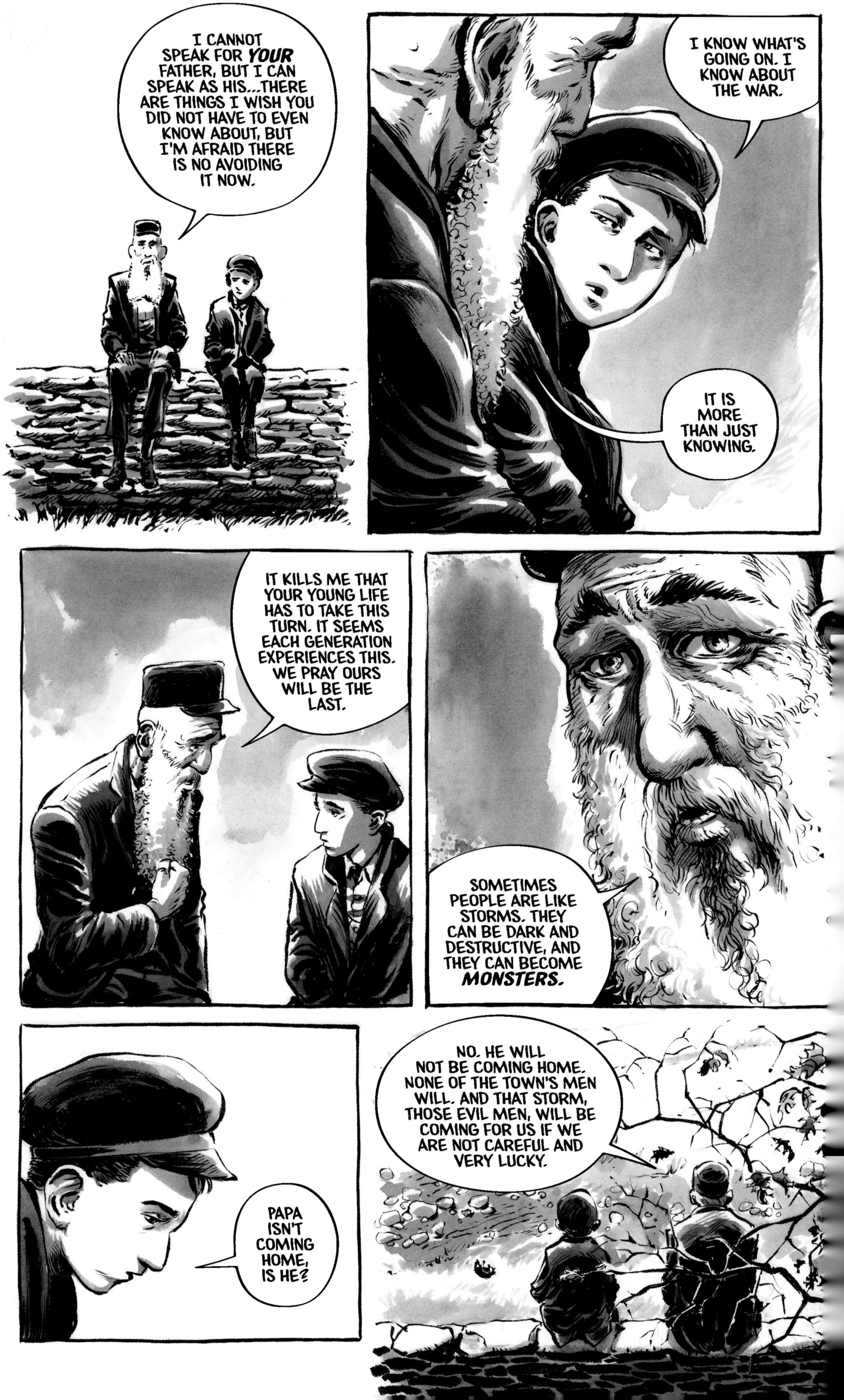
I CANNOT SPEAK FOR YOUR FATHER, BUT I CAN SPEAK AS HIS...THERE ARE THINGS I WISH YOU DID NOT HAVE TO EVEN KNOW ABOUT, BUT I'M AFRAID THERE IS NO AVOIDING IT NOW.
I KNOW WHAT'S GOING ON. I KNOW ABOUT THE WAR.
IT IS MORE THAN JUST KNOWING.
IT KILLS ME THAT YOUR YOUNG LIFE HAS TO TAKE THIS TURN. IT SEEMS EACH GENERATION EXPERIENCES THIS. WE PRAY OURS WILL BE THE LAST.
SOMETIMES PEOPLE ARE LIKE STORMS. THEY CAN BE DARK AND DESTRUCTIVE, AND THEY CAN BECOME MONSTERS.
PAPA ISN'T COMING HOME, IS HE?
NO. HE WILL NOT BE COMING HOME. NONE OF THE TOWN'S MEN WILL. AND THAT STORM, THOSE EVIL MEN, WILL BE COMING FOR US IF WE ARE NOT CAREFUL AND VERY LUCKY.

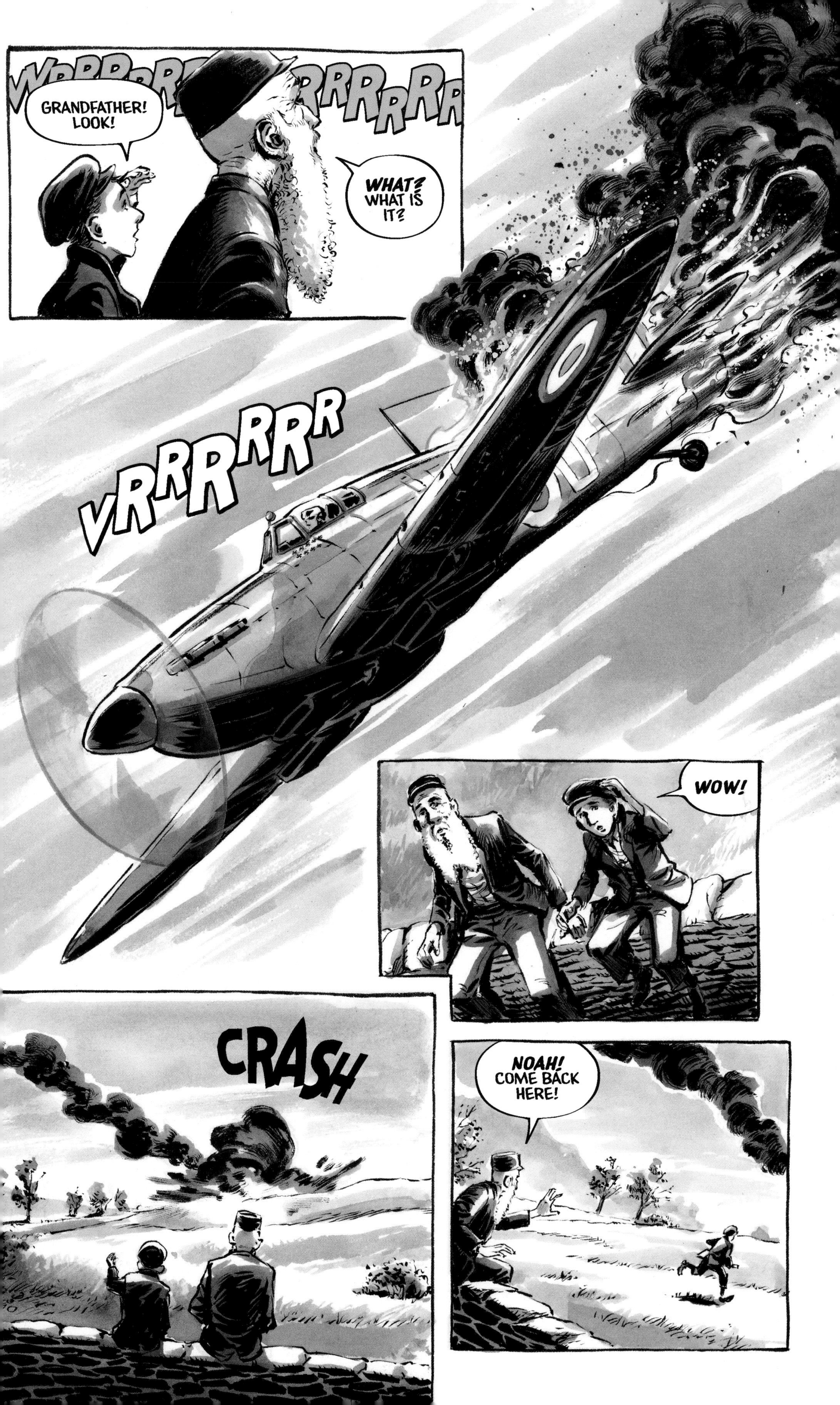
WRRRRRRRRRRRRR
GRANDFATHER! LOOK!
WHAT? WHAT IS IT?
VRRRRRR
WOW!
CRASH
NOAH! COME BACK HERE!

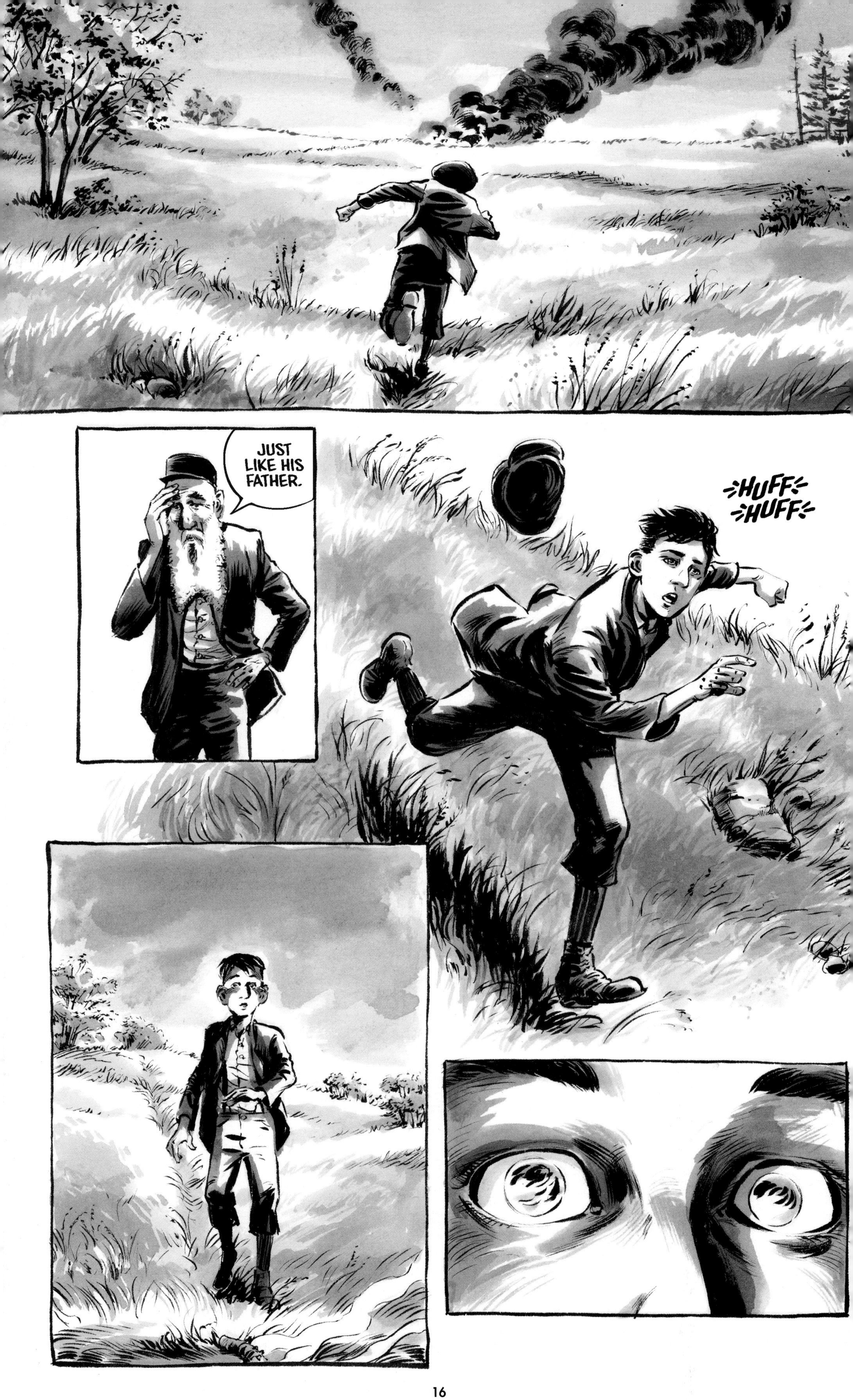
JUST LIKE HIS FATHER.
HUFF HUFF

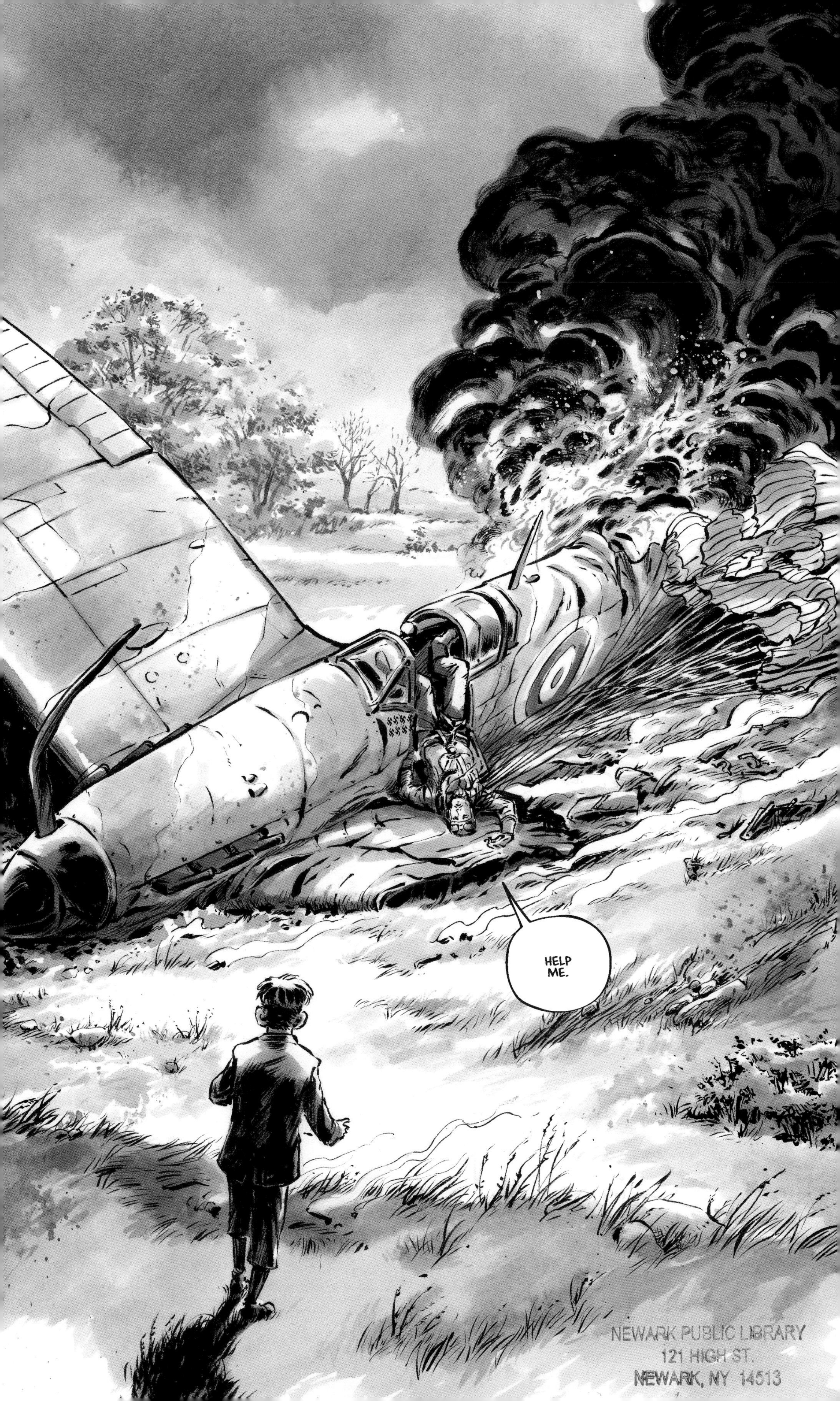
HELP ME.

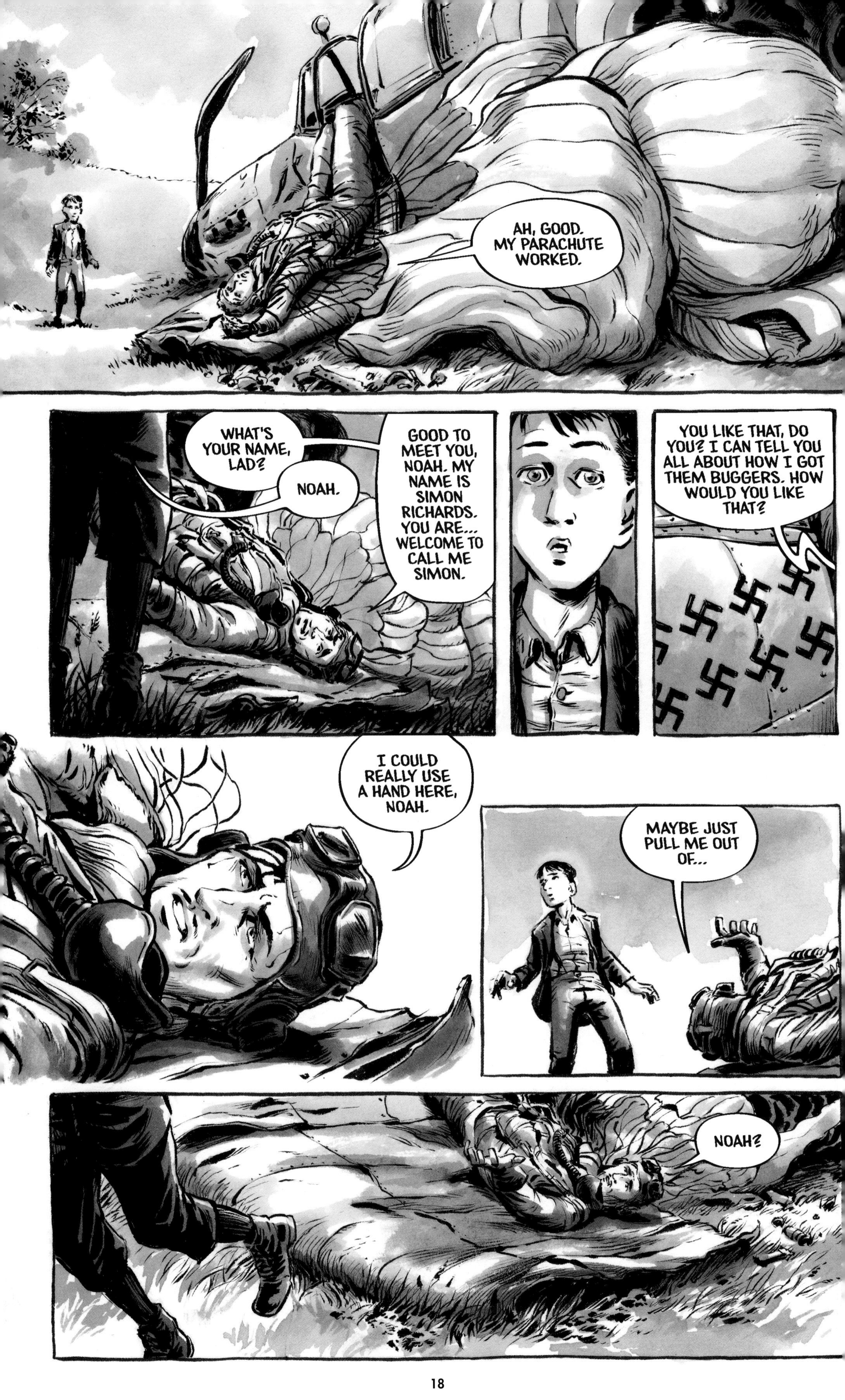
AH, GOOD. MY PARACHUTE WORKED.
WHAT'S YOUR NAME, LAD?
NOAH.
GOOD TO MEET YOU, NOAH. MY NAME IS SIMON RICHARDS. YOU ARE... WELCOME TO CALL ME SIMON.
YOU LIKE THAT, DO YOU? I CAN TELL YOU ALL ABOUT HOW I GOT THEM BUGGERS. HOW WOULD YOU LIKE THAT?
I COULD REALLY USE A HAND HERE, NOAH.
MAYBE JUST PULL ME OUT OF...
NOAH?

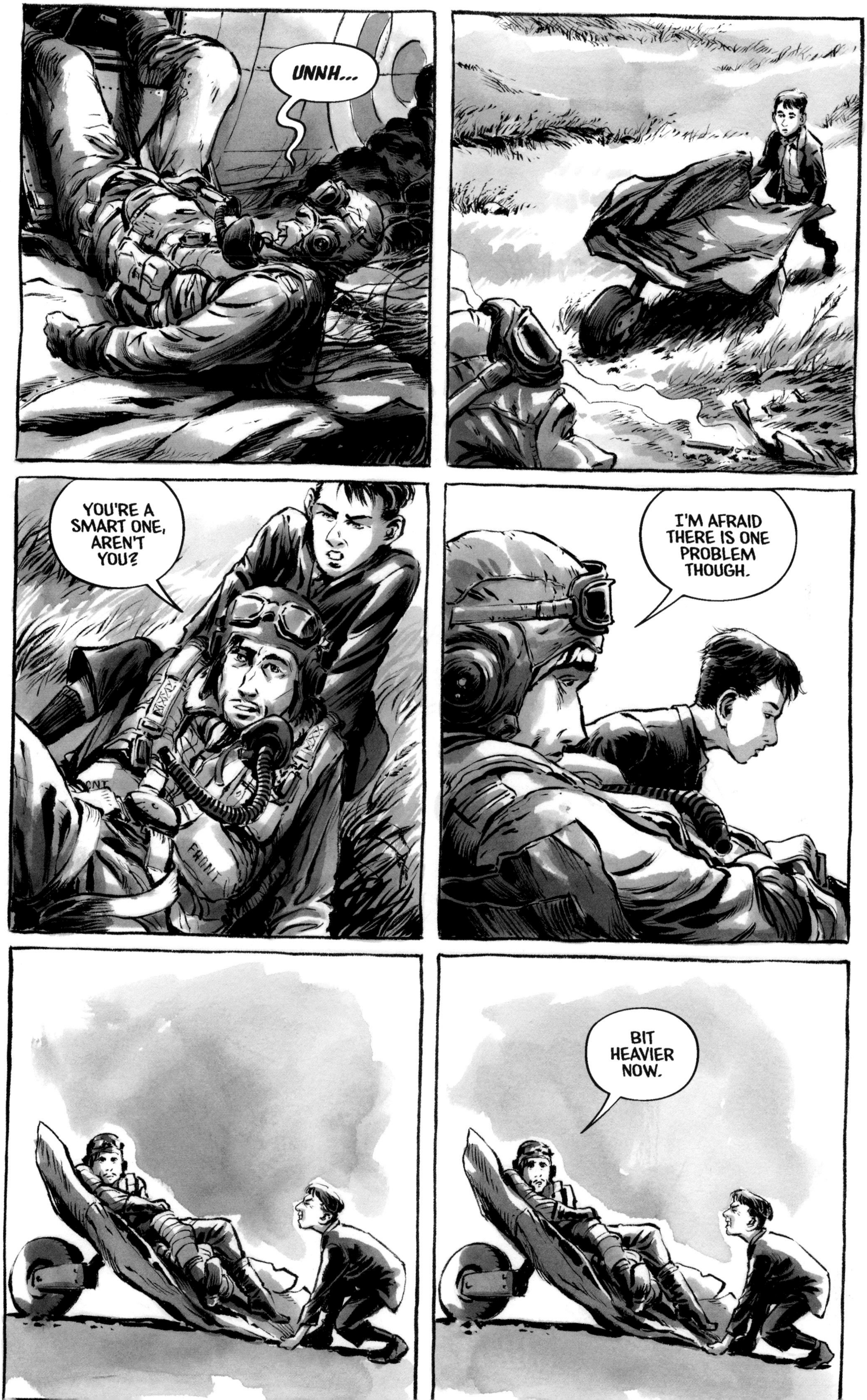
UNNH...
YOU'RE A SMART ONE, AREN'T YOU?
I'M AFRAID THERE IS ONE PROBLEM THOUGH.
BIT HEAVIER NOW.

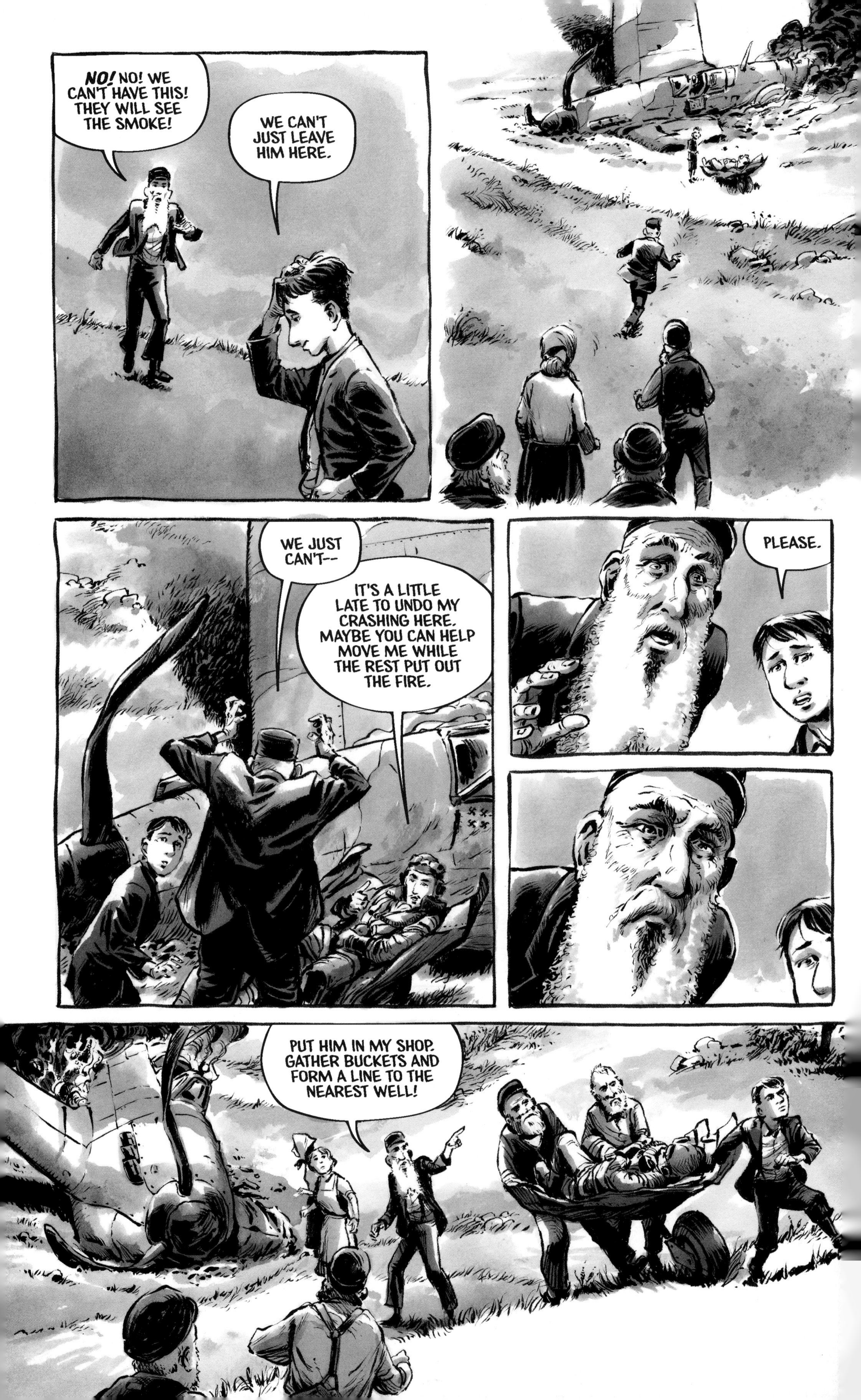
NO! NO! WE CAN'T HAVE THIS! THEY WILL SEE THE SMOKE!
WE CAN'T JUST LEAVE HIM HERE.
WE JUST CAN'T--
IT'S A LITTLE LATE TO UNDO MY CRASHING HERE. MAYBE YOU CAN HELP MOVE ME WHILE THE REST PUT OUT THE FIRE.
PLEASE.
PUT HIM IN MY SHOP. GATHER BUCKETS AND FORM A LINE TO THE NEAREST WELL!

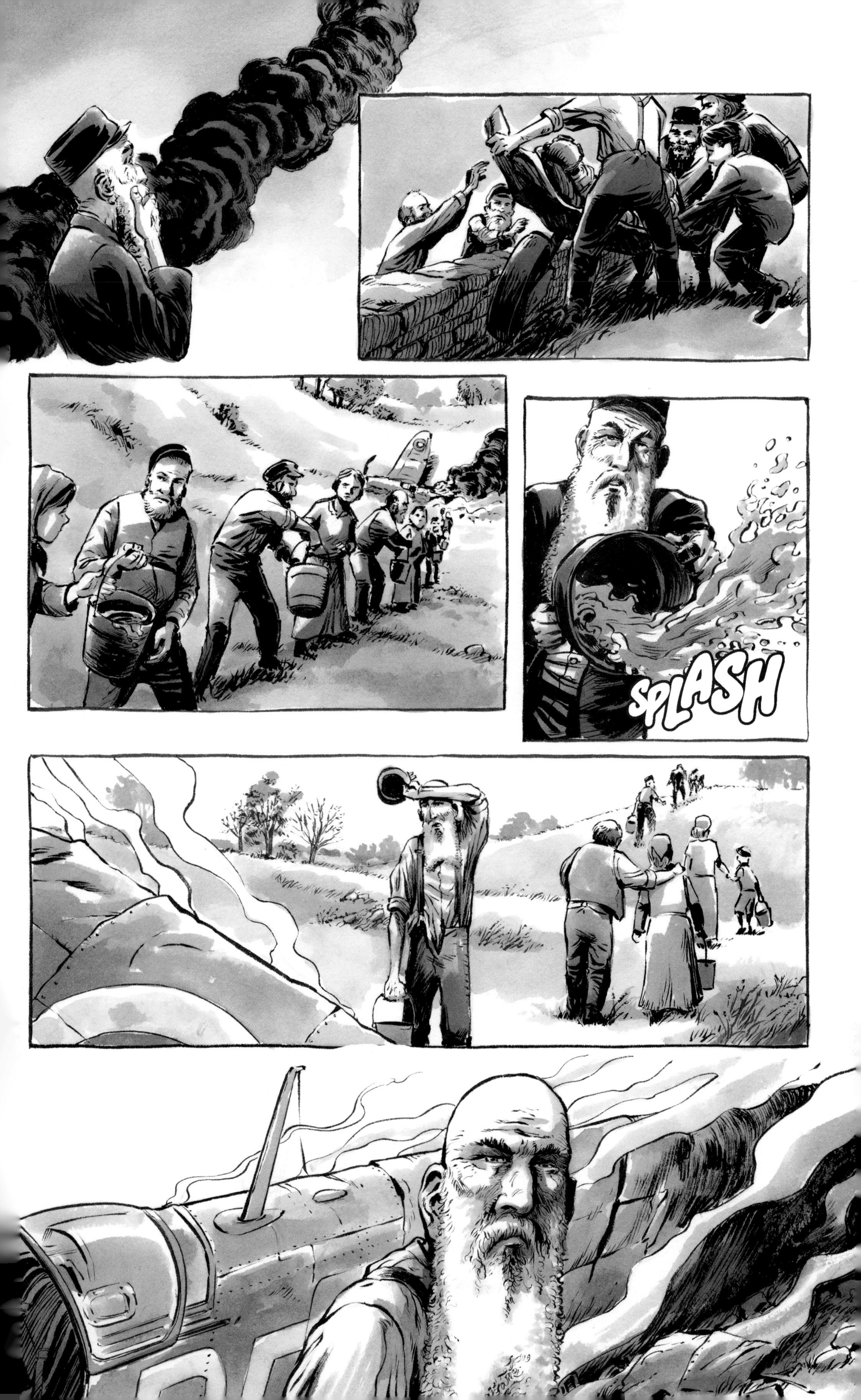
SPLASH

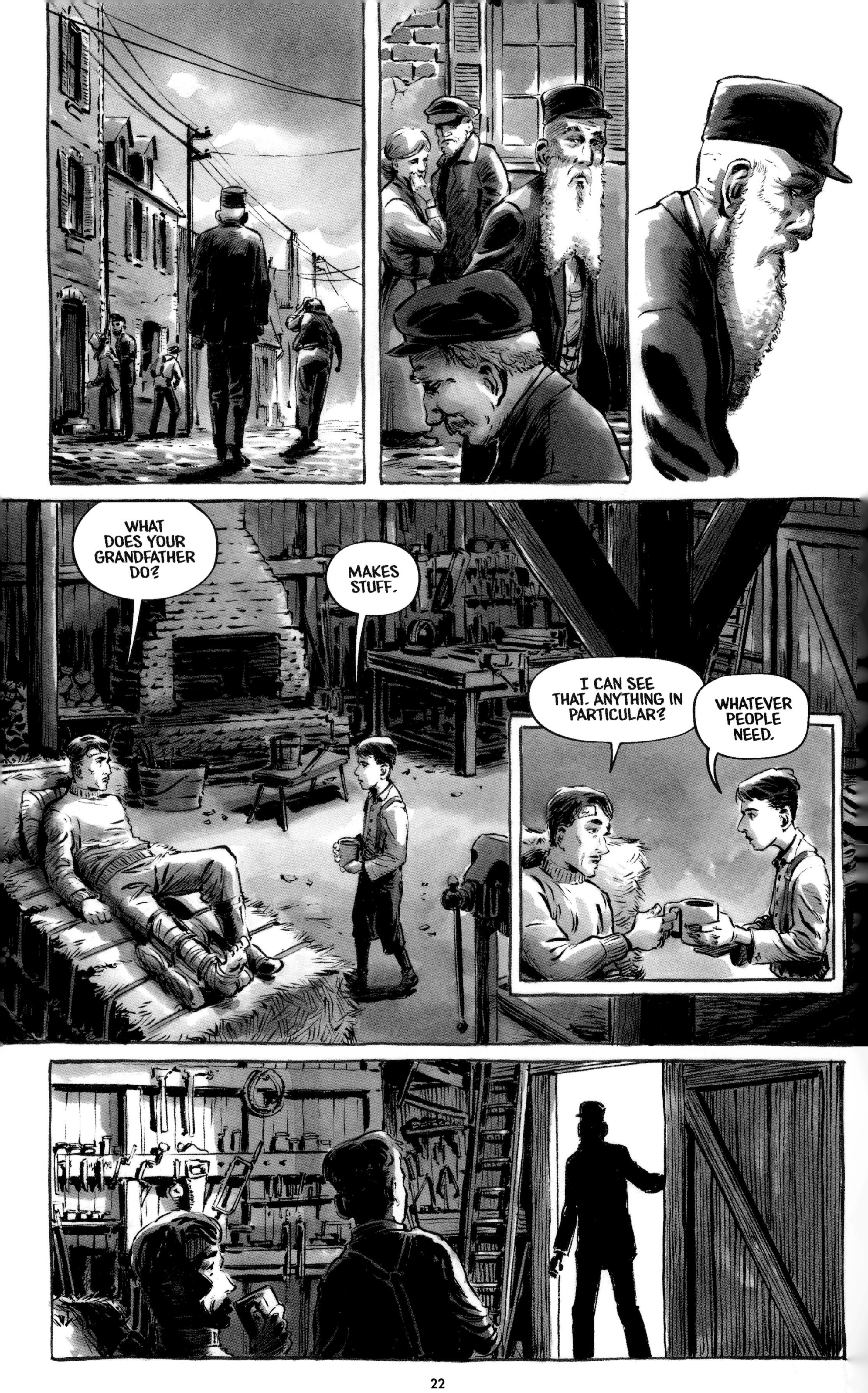
WHAT DOES YOUR GRANDFATHER DO?
MAKES STUFF.
I CAN SEE THAT. ANYTHING IN PARTICULAR?
WHATEVER PEOPLE NEED.

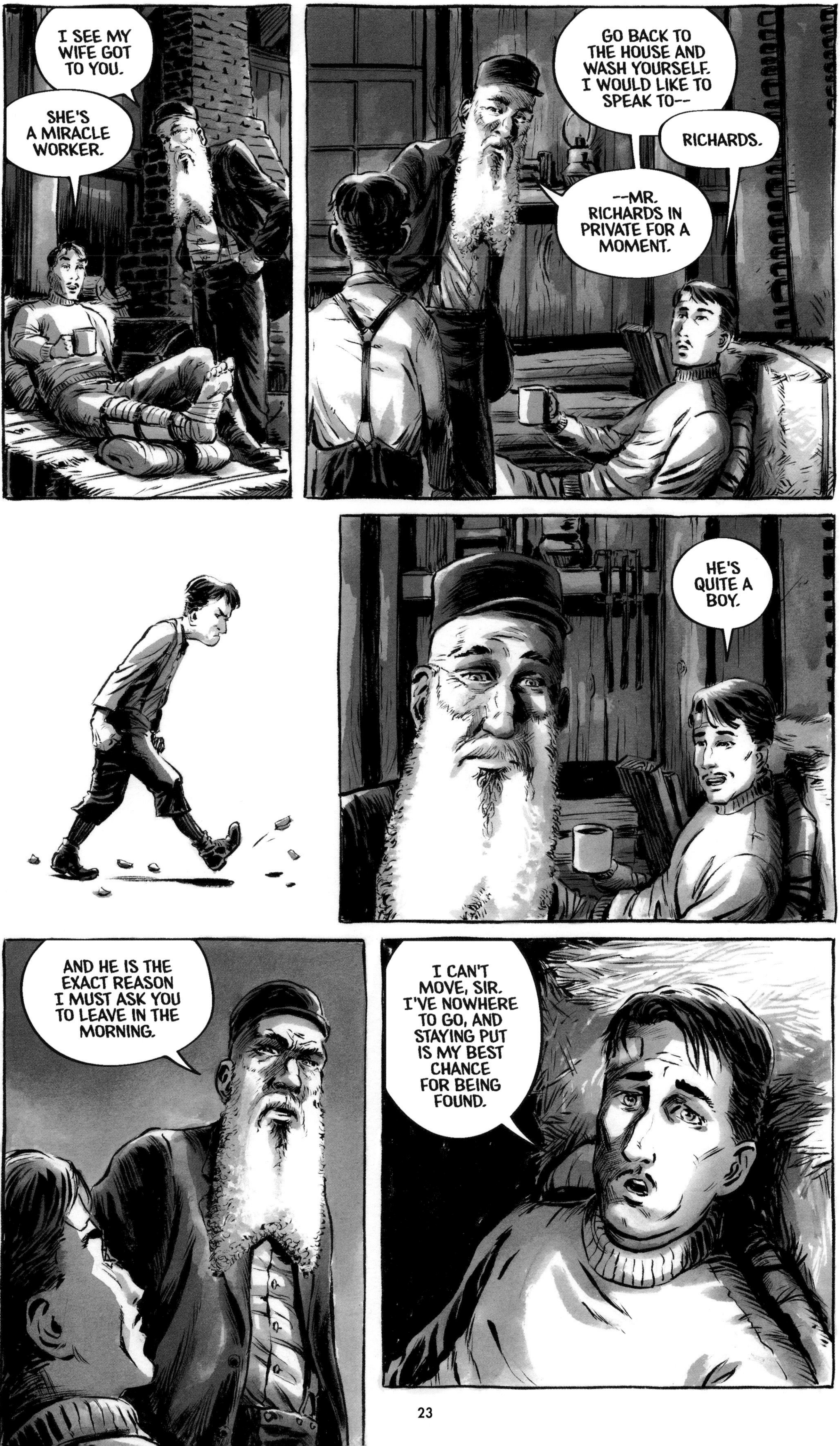
I SEE MY WIFE GOT TO YOU.
SHE'S A MIRACLE WORKER.
GO BACK TO THE HOUSE AND WASH YOURSELF. I WOULD LIKE TO SPEAK TO--
RICHARDS.
--MR. RICHARDS IN PRIVATE FOR A MOMENT.
HE'S QUITE A BOY.
AND HE IS THE EXACT REASON I MUST ASK YOU TO LEAVE IN THE MORNING.
I CAN'T MOVE, SIR. I'VE NOWHERE TO GO, AND STAYING PUT IS MY BEST CHANCE FOR BEING FOUND.

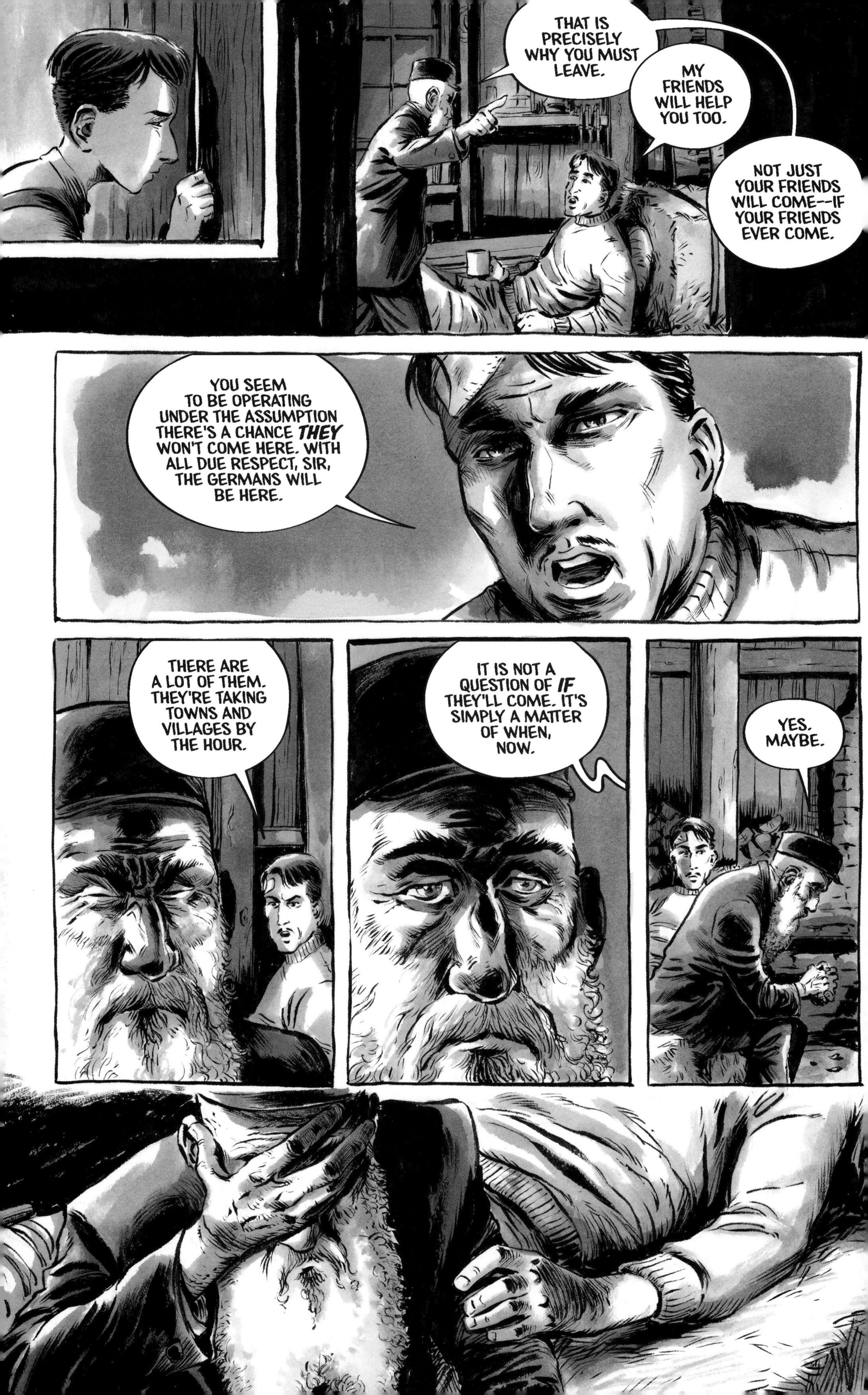
THAT IS PRECISELY WHY YOU MUST LEAVE.
MY FRIENDS WILL HELP YOU TOO.
NOT JUST YOUR FRIENDS WILL COME--IF YOUR FRIENDS EVER COME.
YOU SEEM TO BE OPERATING UNDER THE ASSUMPTION THERE'S A CHANCE *THEY* WON'T COME HERE. WITH ALL DUE RESPECT, SIR, THE GERMANS WILL BE HERE.
THERE ARE A LOT OF THEM. THEY'RE TAKING TOWNS AND VILLAGES BY THE HOUR.
IT IS NOT A QUESTION OF *IF* THEY'LL COME. IT'S SIMPLY A MATTER OF WHEN, NOW.
YES. MAYBE.

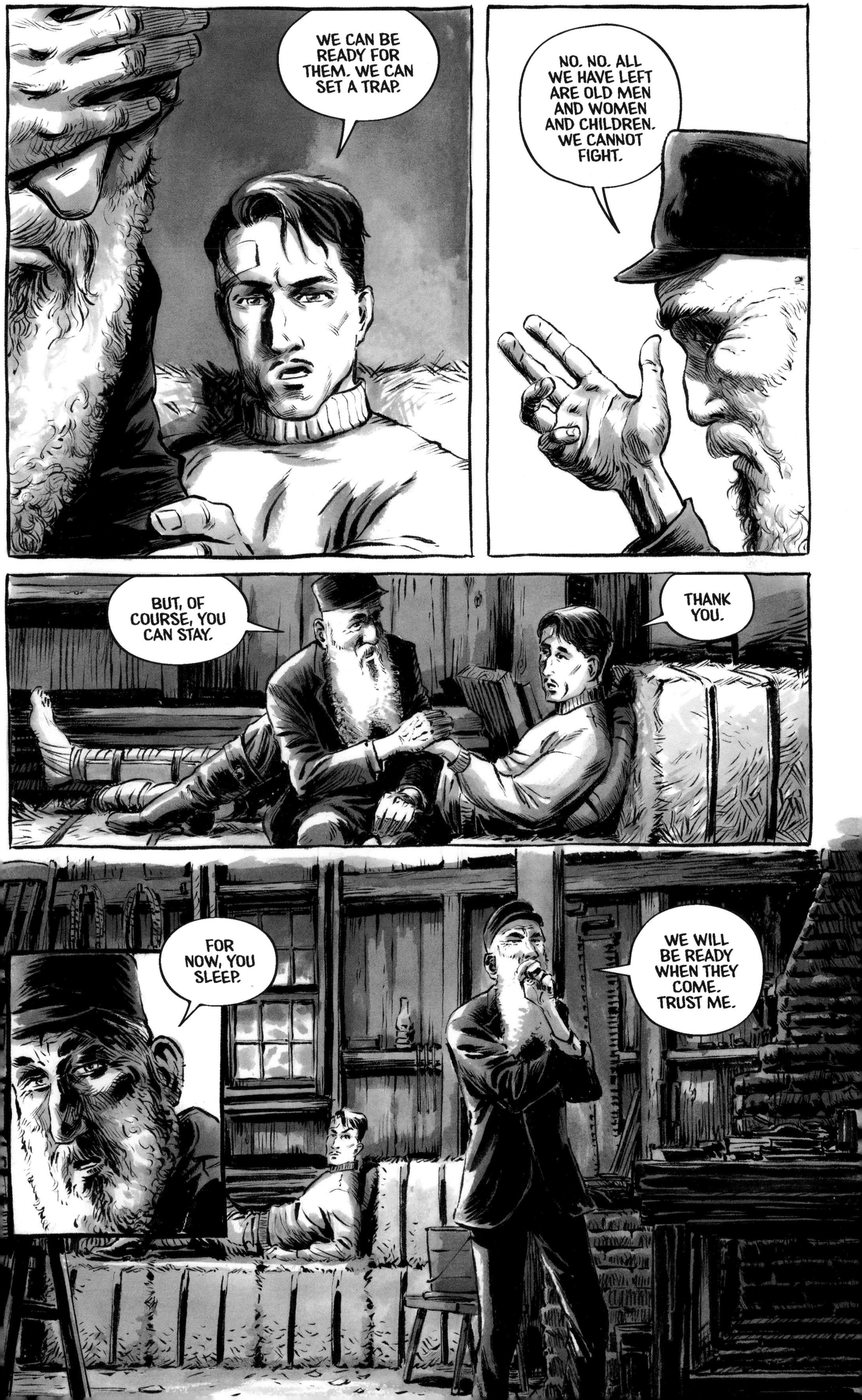
WE CAN BE READY FOR THEM. WE CAN SET A TRAP.
NO. NO. ALL WE HAVE LEFT ARE OLD MEN AND WOMEN AND CHILDREN. WE CANNOT FIGHT.
BUT, OF COURSE, YOU CAN STAY.
THANK YOU.
FOR NOW, YOU SLEEP.
WE WILL BE READY WHEN THEY COME. TRUST ME.

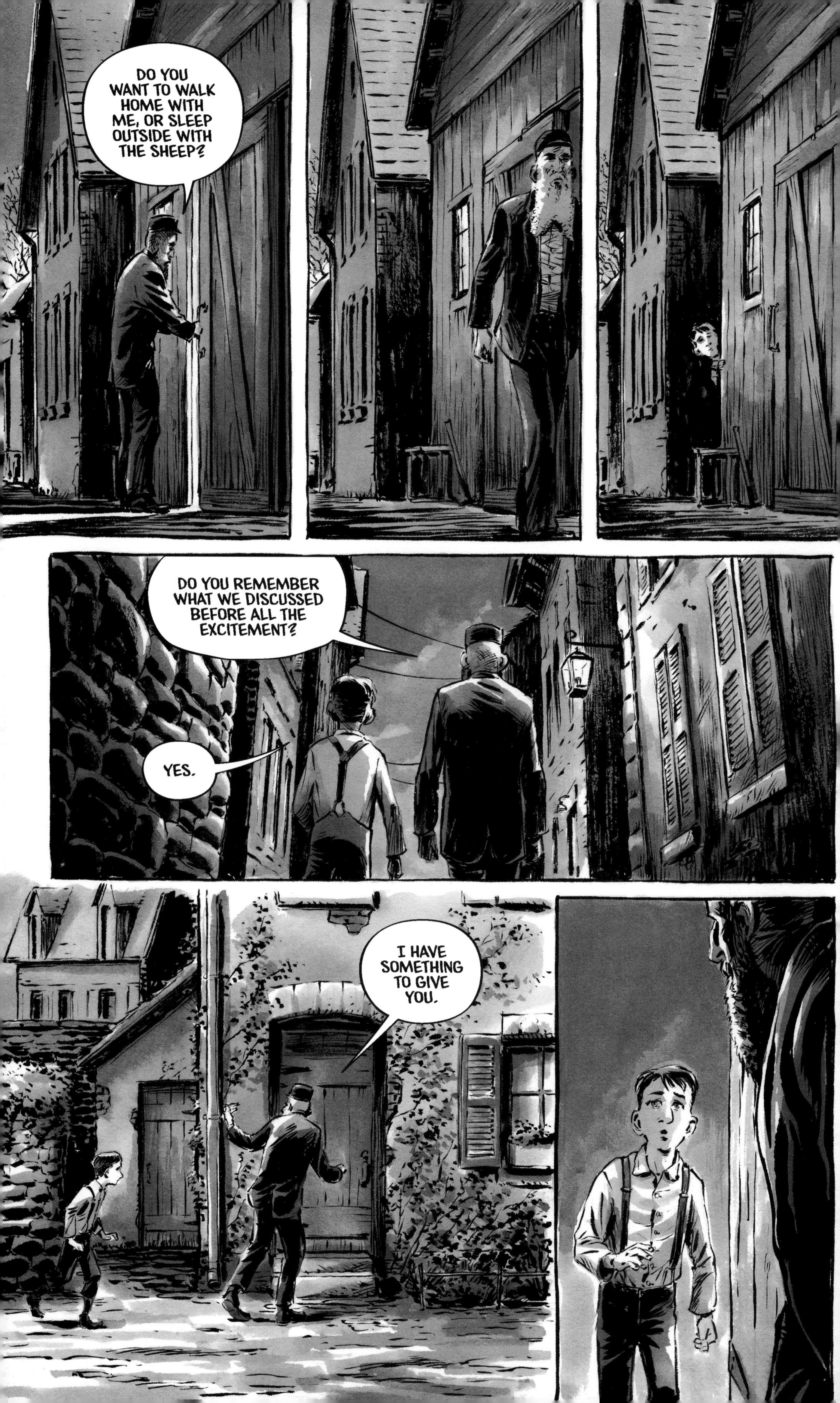
DO YOU WANT TO WALK HOME WITH ME, OR SLEEP OUTSIDE WITH THE SHEEP?
DO YOU REMEMBER WHAT WE DISCUSSED BEFORE ALL THE EXCITEMENT?
YES.
I HAVE SOMETHING TO GIVE YOU.

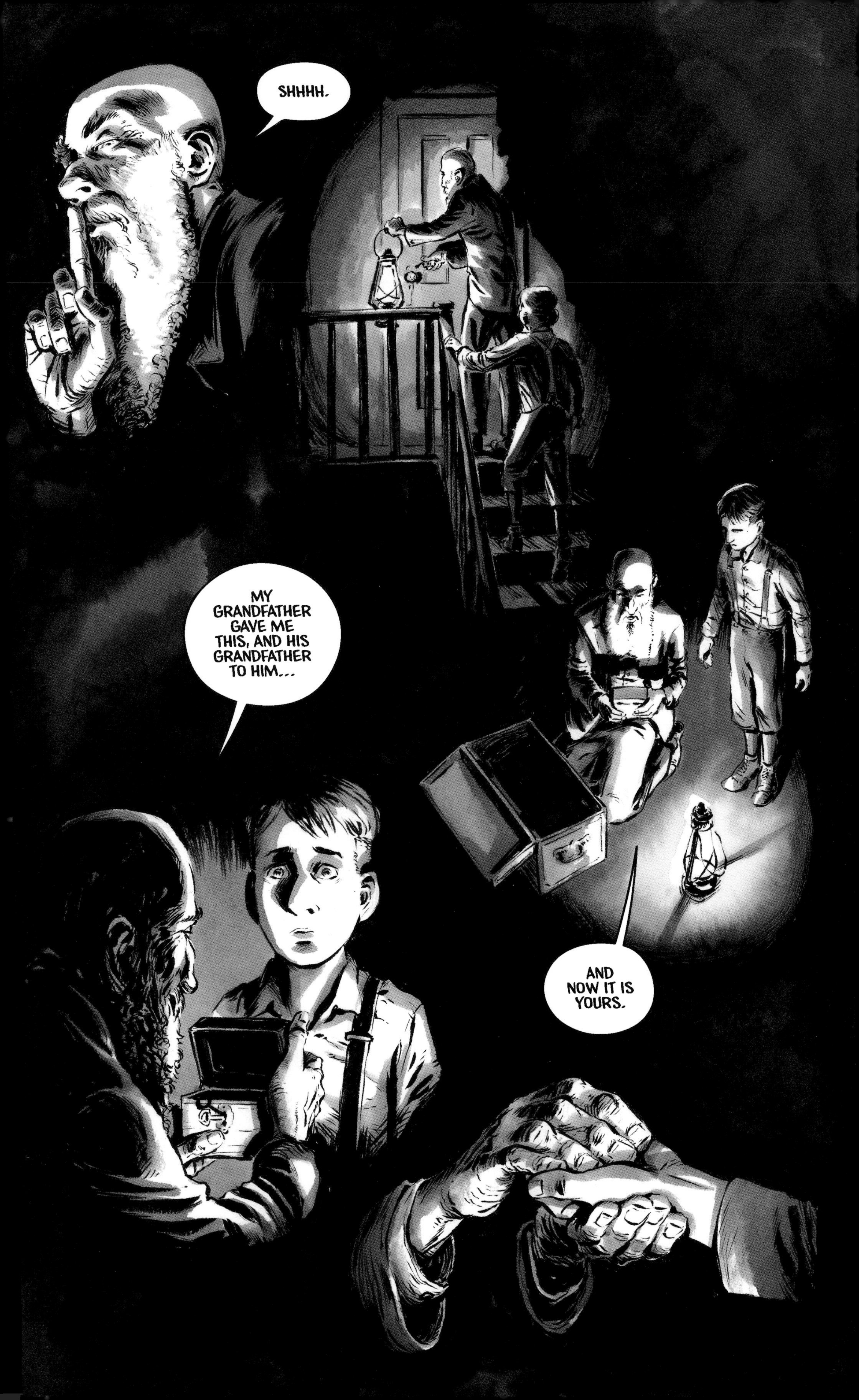
SHHHH.
MY GRANDFATHER GAVE ME THIS, AND HIS GRANDFATHER TO HIM...
AND NOW IT IS YOURS.

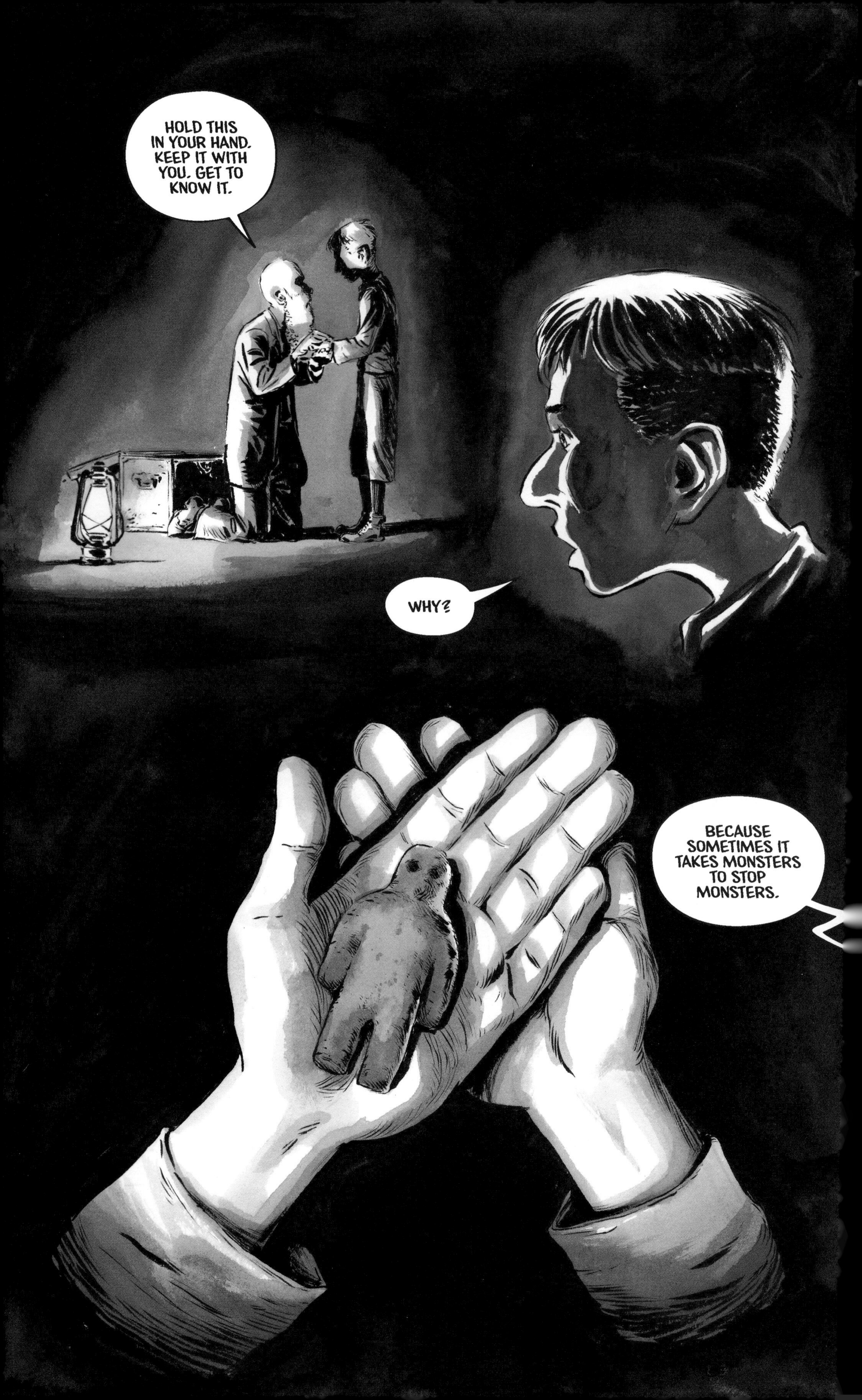
HOLD THIS IN YOUR HAND. KEEP IT WITH YOU. GET TO KNOW IT.
WHY?
BECAUSE SOMETIMES IT TAKES MONSTERS TO STOP MONSTERS.

CHAPTER TWO

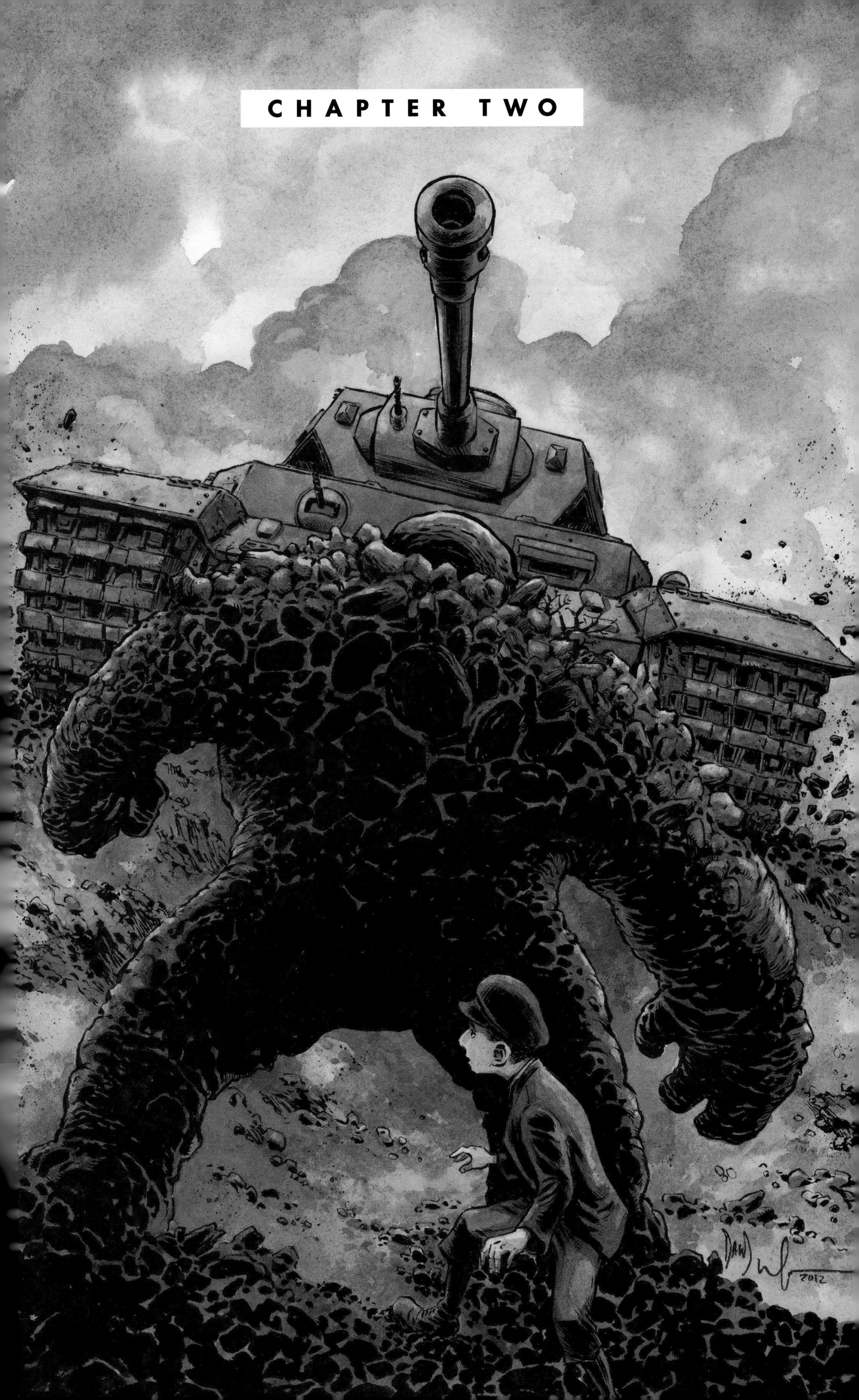

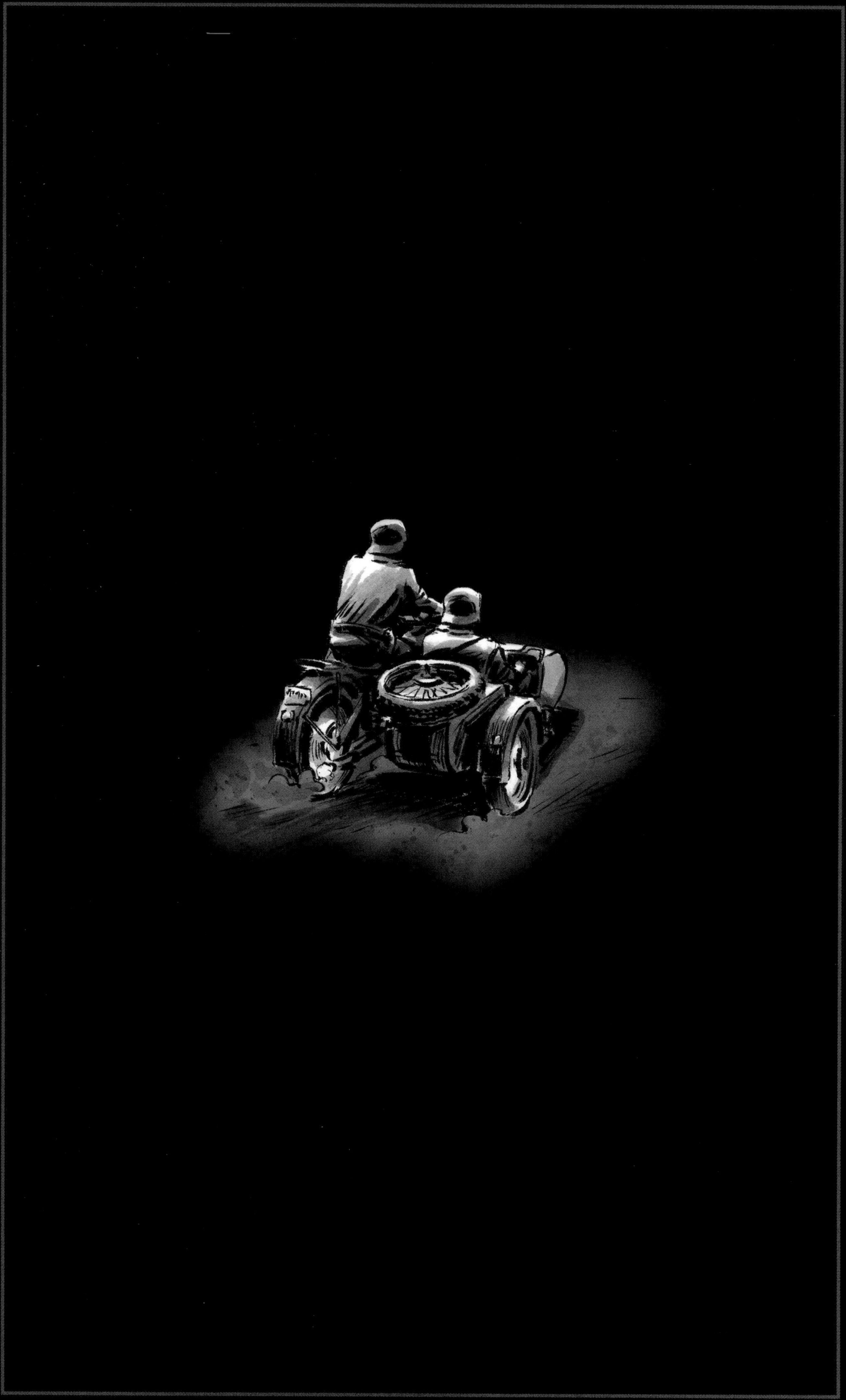

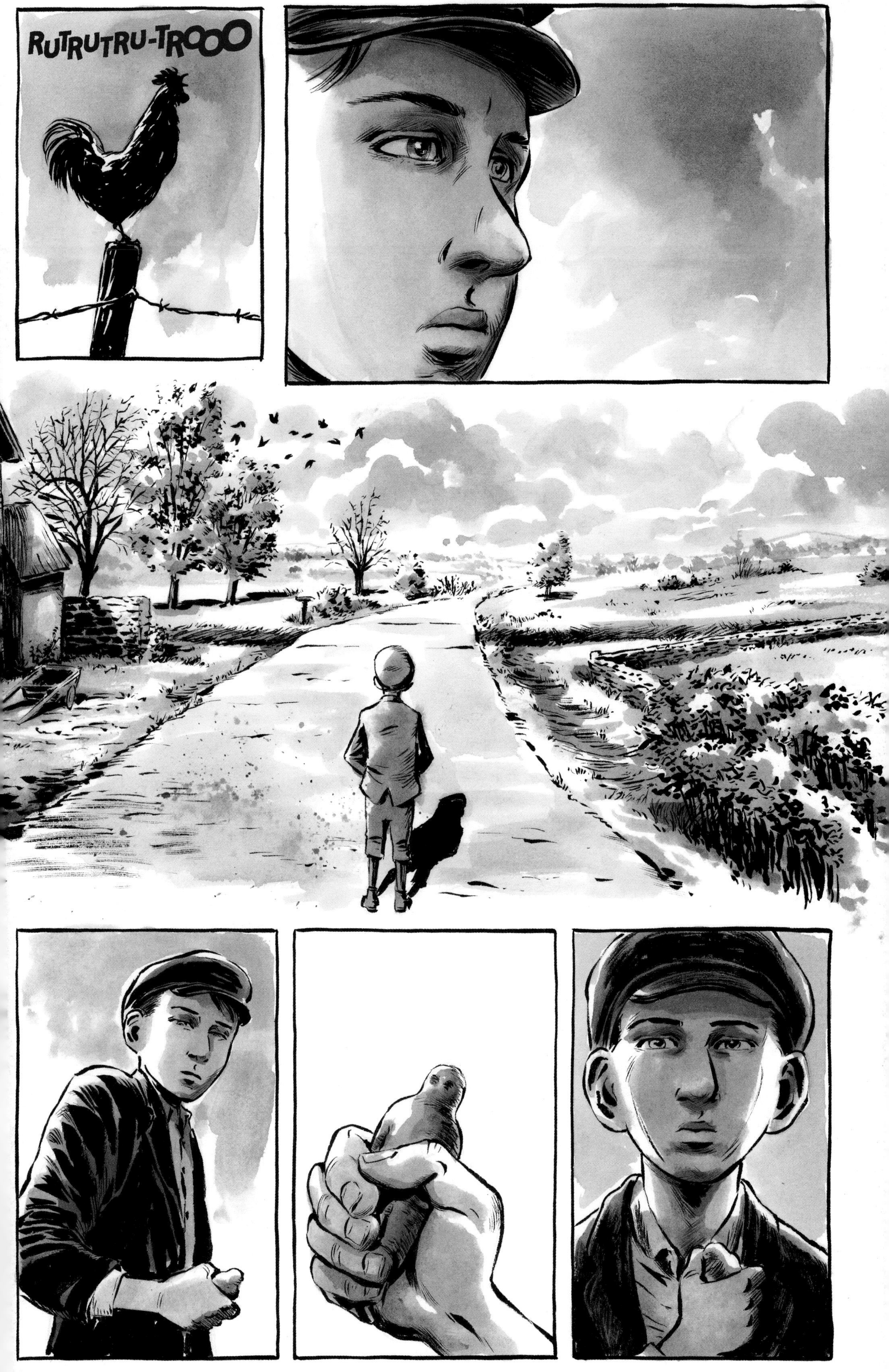
RUTRUTRU-TROOO

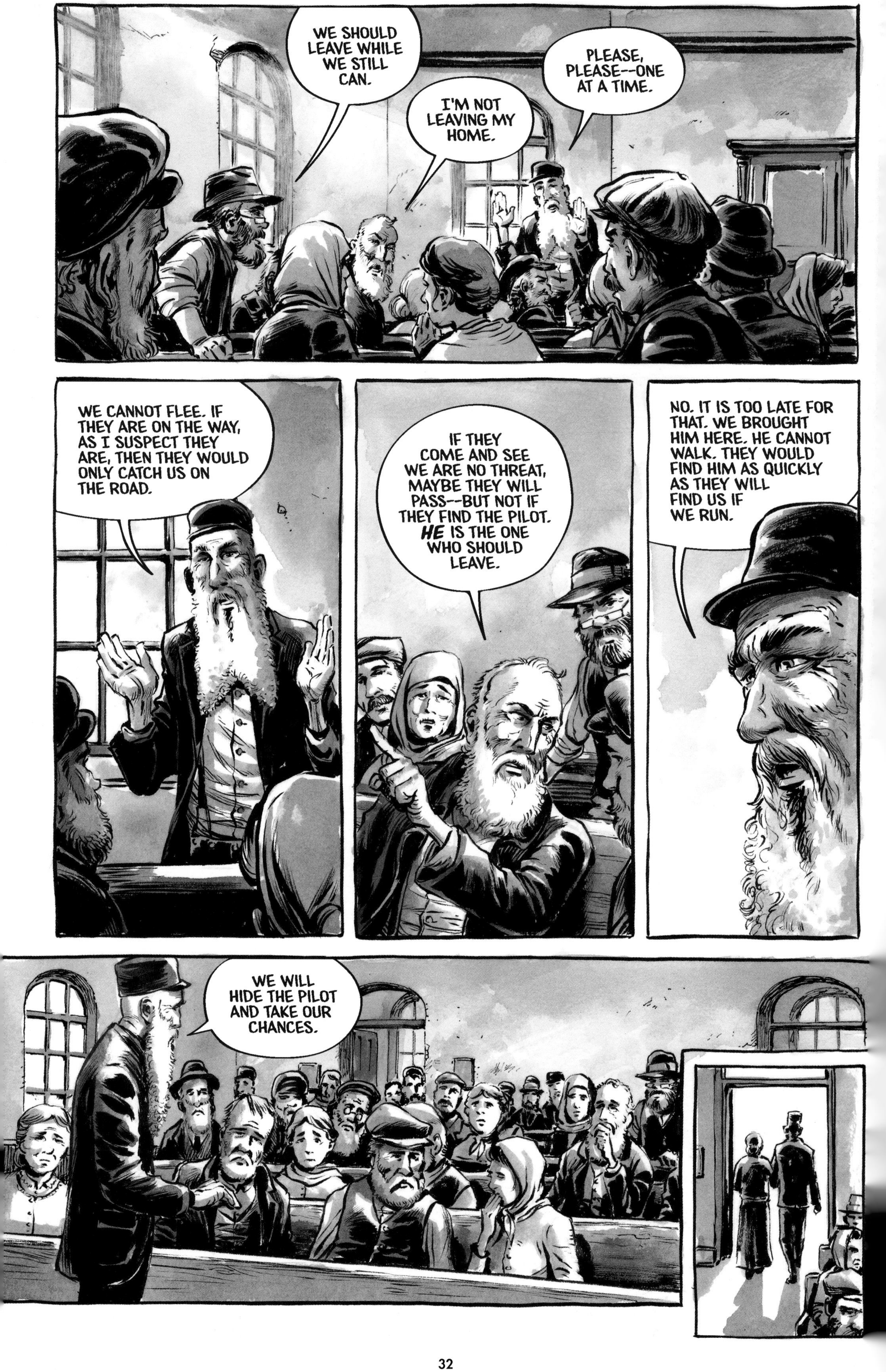
WE SHOULD LEAVE WHILE WE STILL CAN.
I'M NOT LEAVING MY HOME.
PLEASE, PLEASE--ONE AT A TIME.
WE CANNOT FLEE. IF THEY ARE ON THE WAY, AS I SUSPECT THEY ARE, THEN THEY WOULD ONLY CATCH US ON THE ROAD.
IF THEY COME AND SEE WE ARE NO THREAT, MAYBE THEY WILL PASS--BUT NOT IF THEY FIND THE PILOT. **HE** IS THE ONE WHO SHOULD LEAVE.
NO. IT IS TOO LATE FOR THAT. WE BROUGHT HIM HERE. HE CANNOT WALK. THEY WOULD FIND HIM AS QUICKLY AS THEY WILL FIND US IF WE RUN.
WE WILL HIDE THE PILOT AND TAKE OUR CHANCES.

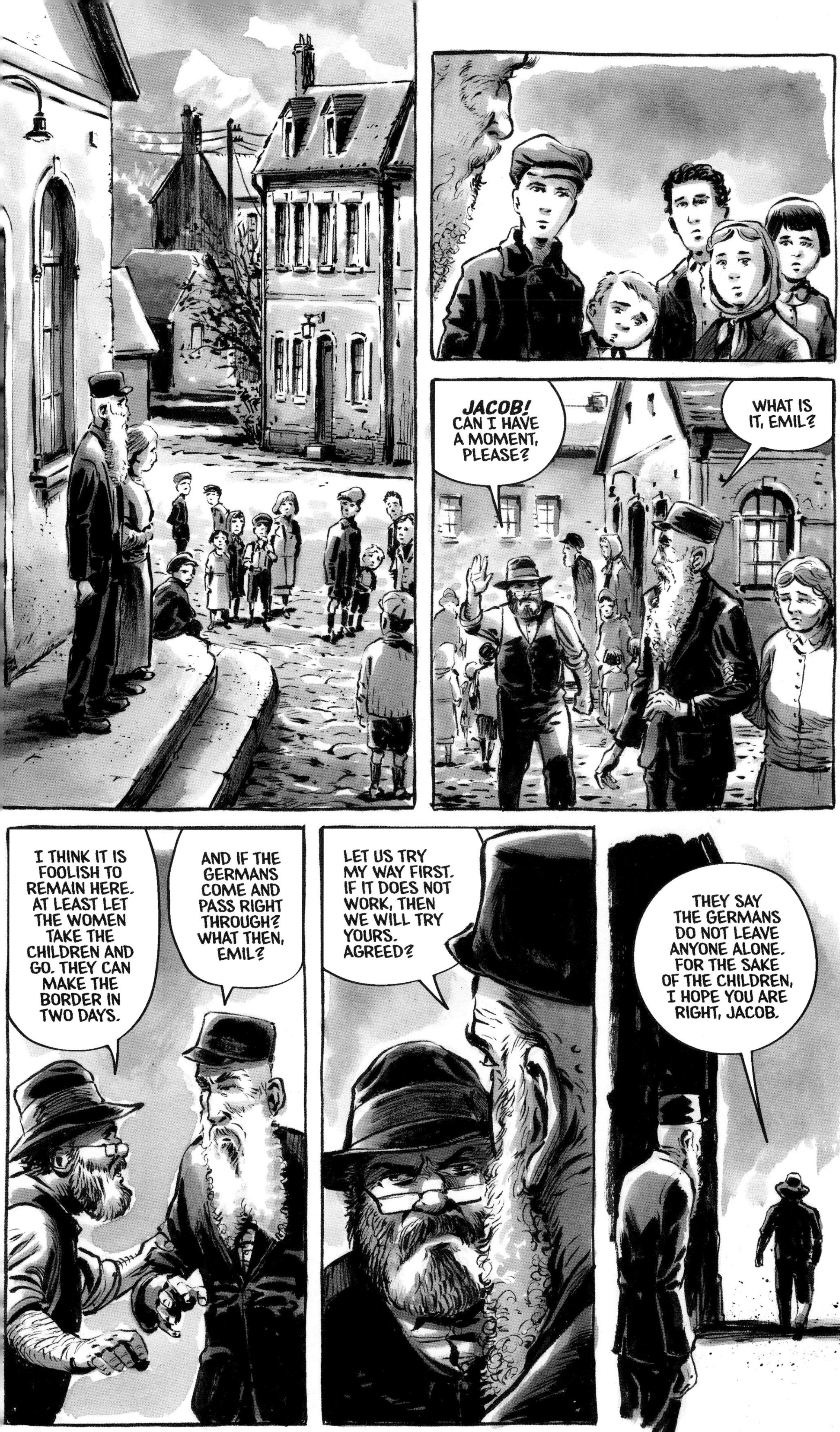
JACOB! CAN I HAVE A MOMENT, PLEASE?
WHAT IS IT, EMIL?
I THINK IT IS FOOLISH TO REMAIN HERE. AT LEAST LET THE WOMEN TAKE THE CHILDREN AND GO. THEY CAN MAKE THE BORDER IN TWO DAYS.
AND IF THE GERMANS COME AND PASS RIGHT THROUGH? WHAT THEN, EMIL?
LET US TRY MY WAY FIRST. IF IT DOES NOT WORK, THEN WE WILL TRY YOURS. AGREED?
THEY SAY THE GERMANS DO NOT LEAVE ANYONE ALONE. FOR THE SAKE OF THE CHILDREN, I HOPE YOU ARE RIGHT, JACOB.

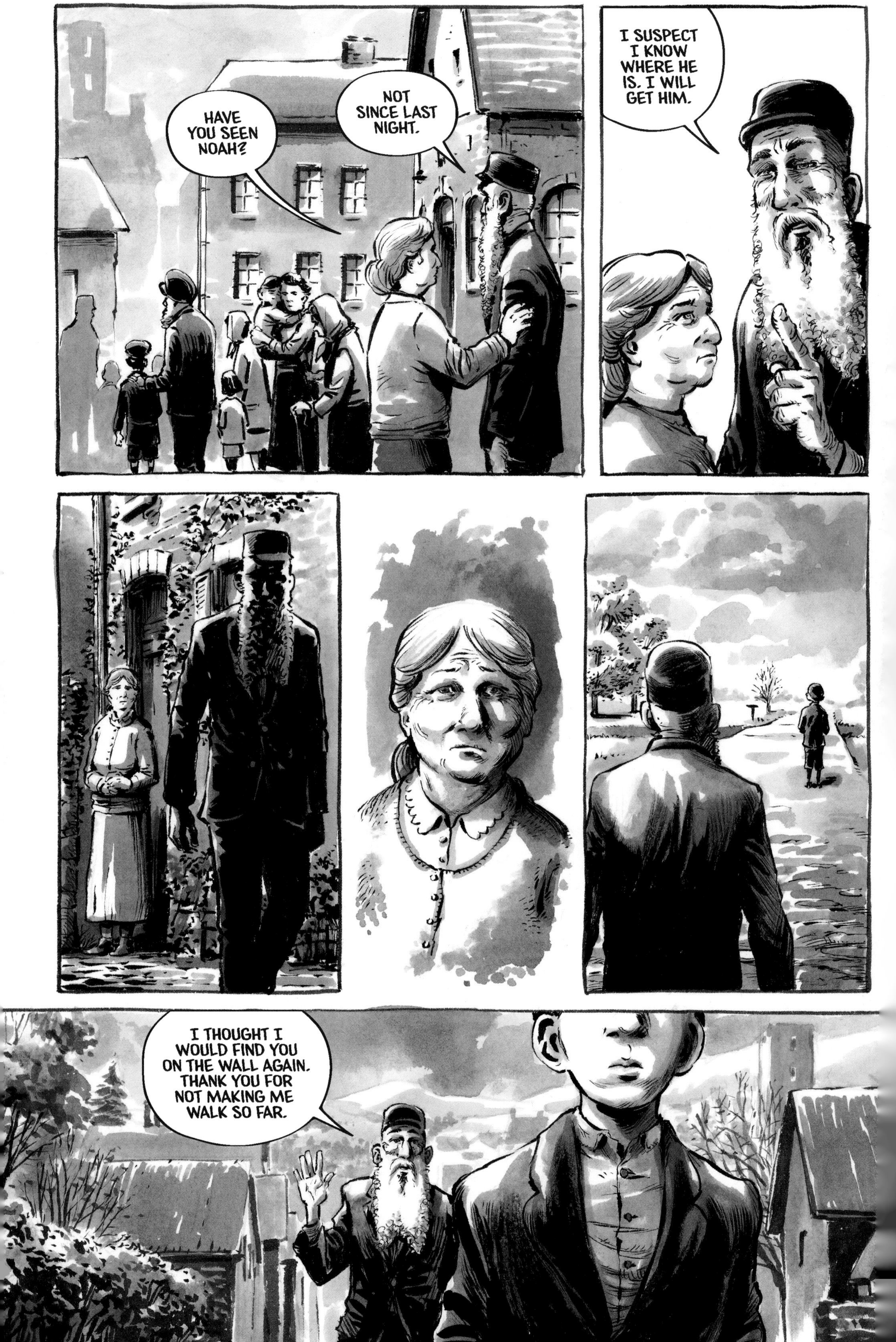
HAVE YOU SEEN NOAH?
NOT SINCE LAST NIGHT.
I SUSPECT I KNOW WHERE HE IS. I WILL GET HIM.
I THOUGHT I WOULD FIND YOU ON THE WALL AGAIN. THANK YOU FOR NOT MAKING ME WALK SO FAR.

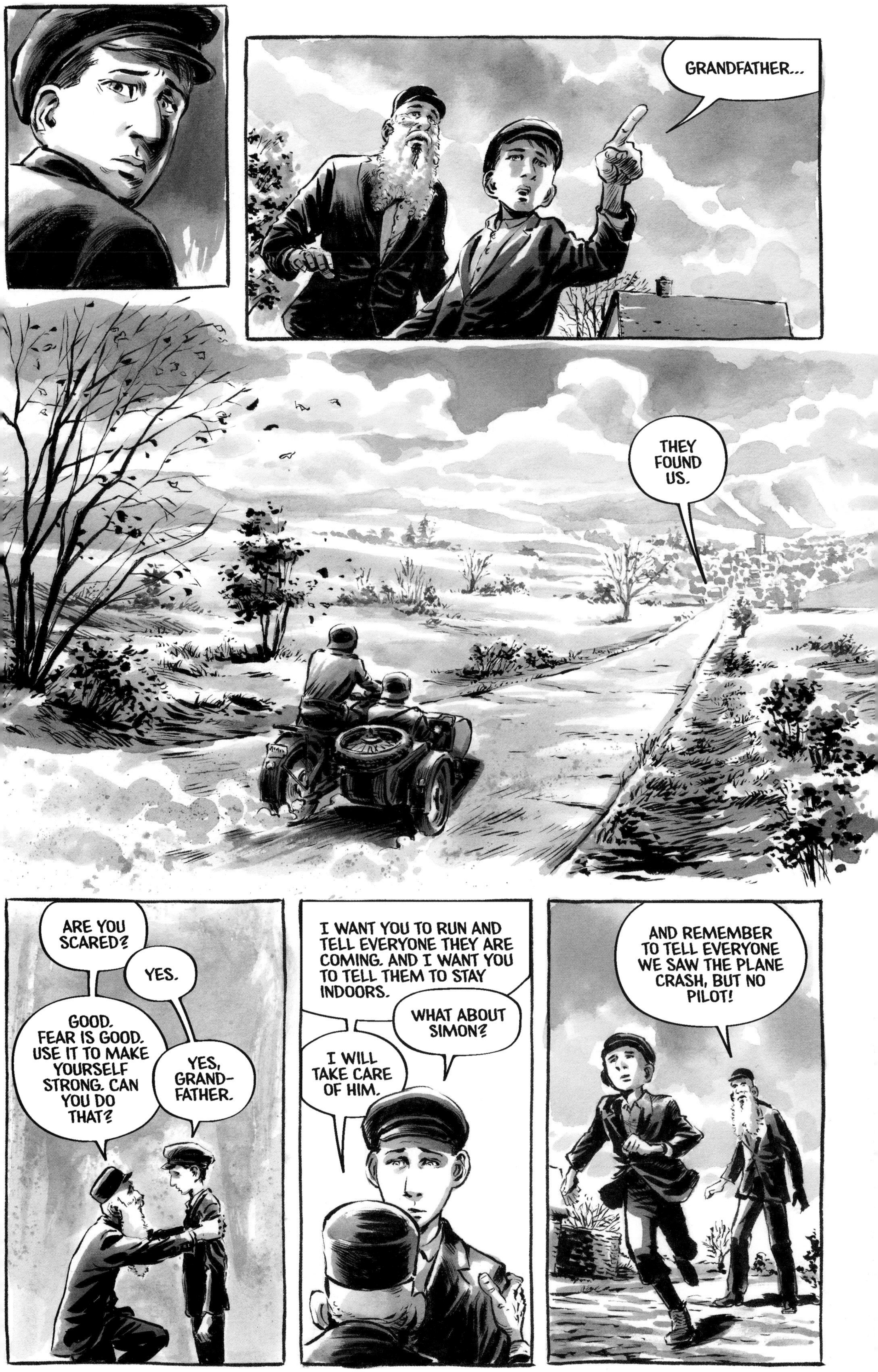
GRANDFATHER...
THEY FOUND US.
ARE YOU SCARED?
YES.
GOOD. FEAR IS GOOD. USE IT TO MAKE YOURSELF STRONG. CAN YOU DO THAT?
YES, GRAND-FATHER.
I WANT YOU TO RUN AND TELL EVERYONE THEY ARE COMING. AND I WANT YOU TO TELL THEM TO STAY INDOORS.
WHAT ABOUT SIMON?
I WILL TAKE CARE OF HIM.
AND REMEMBER TO TELL EVERYONE WE SAW THE PLANE CRASH, BUT NO PILOT!

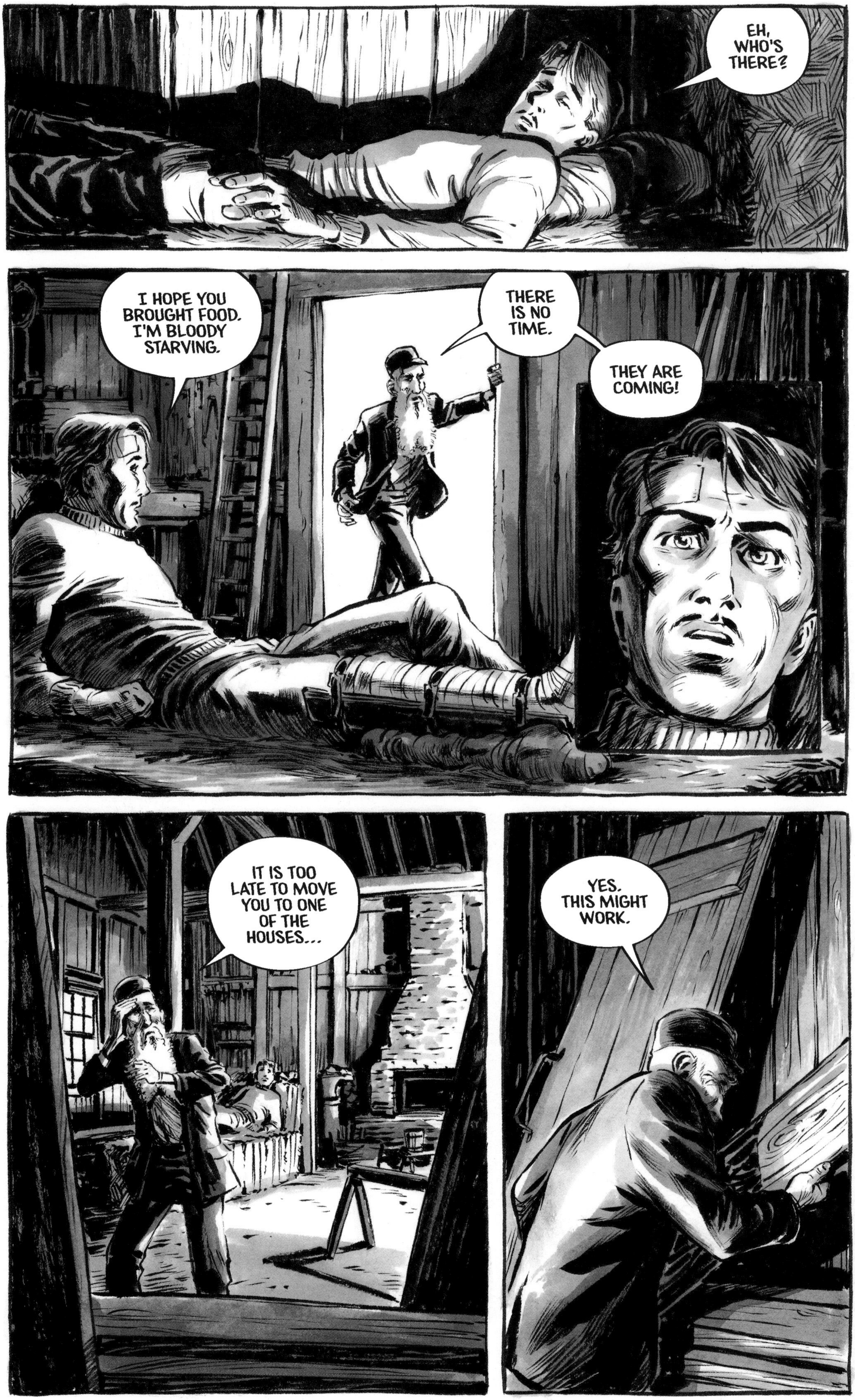
EH, WHO'S THERE?
I HOPE YOU BROUGHT FOOD. I'M BLOODY STARVING.
THERE IS NO TIME.
THEY ARE COMING!
IT IS TOO LATE TO MOVE YOU TO ONE OF THE HOUSES...
YES. THIS MIGHT WORK.

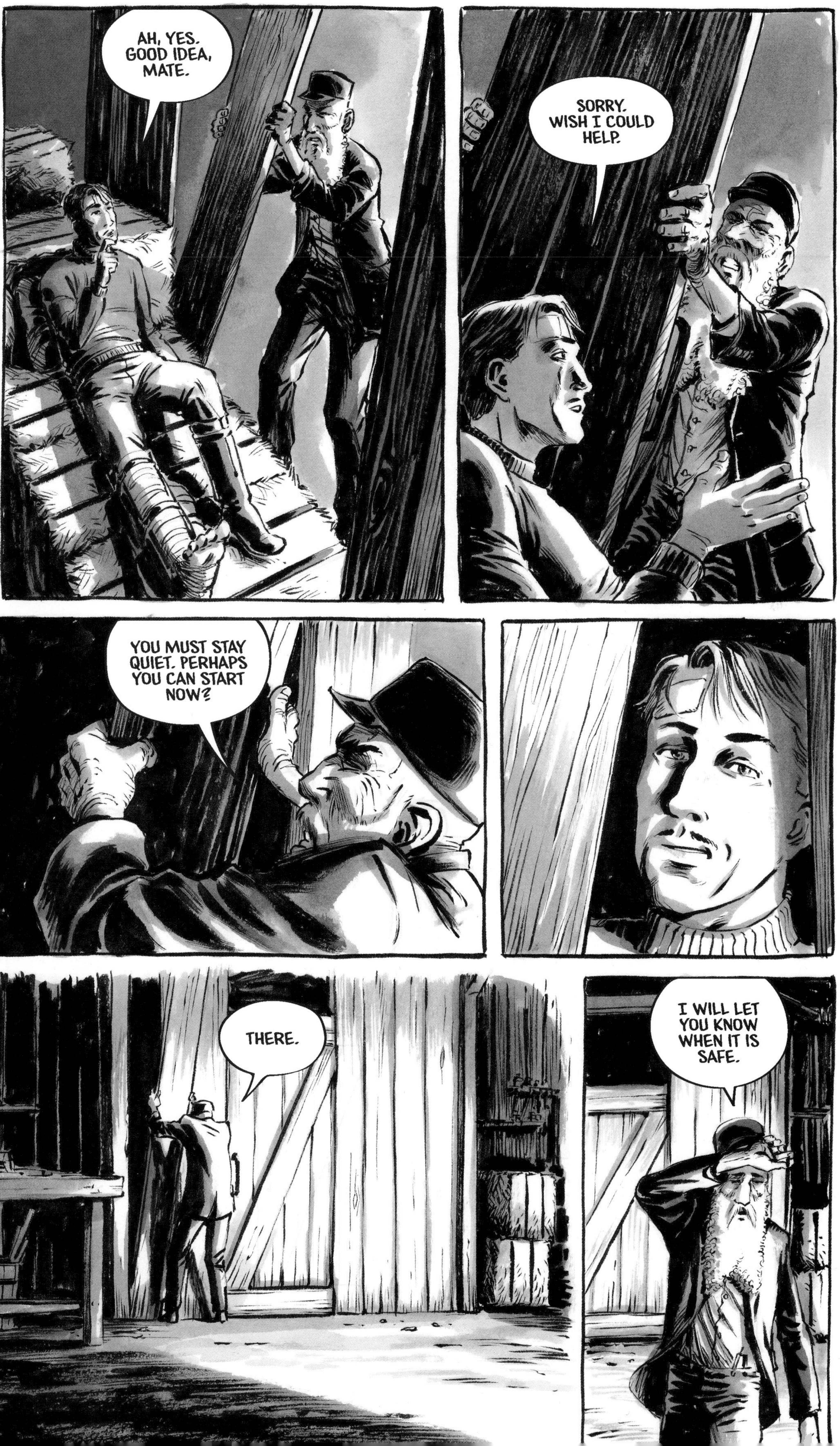
AH, YES. GOOD IDEA, MATE.
SORRY. WISH I COULD HELP.
YOU MUST STAY QUIET. PERHAPS YOU CAN START NOW?
THERE.
I WILL LET YOU KNOW WHEN IT IS SAFE.

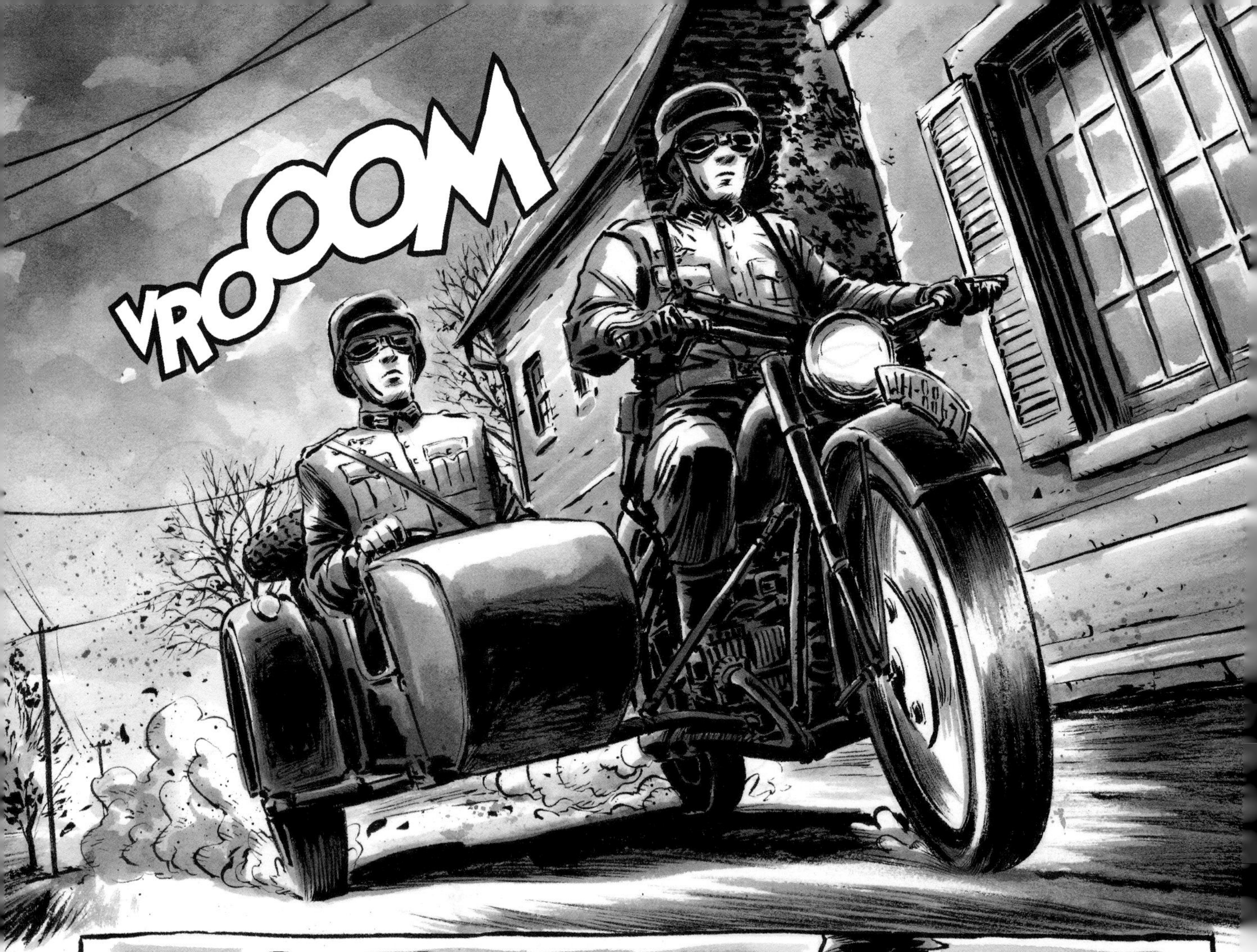
VROOOOM

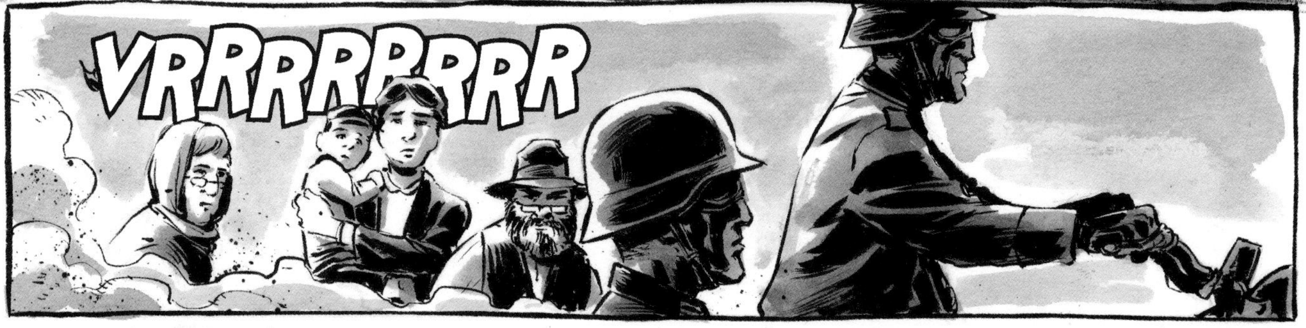
VRRRRRRRR

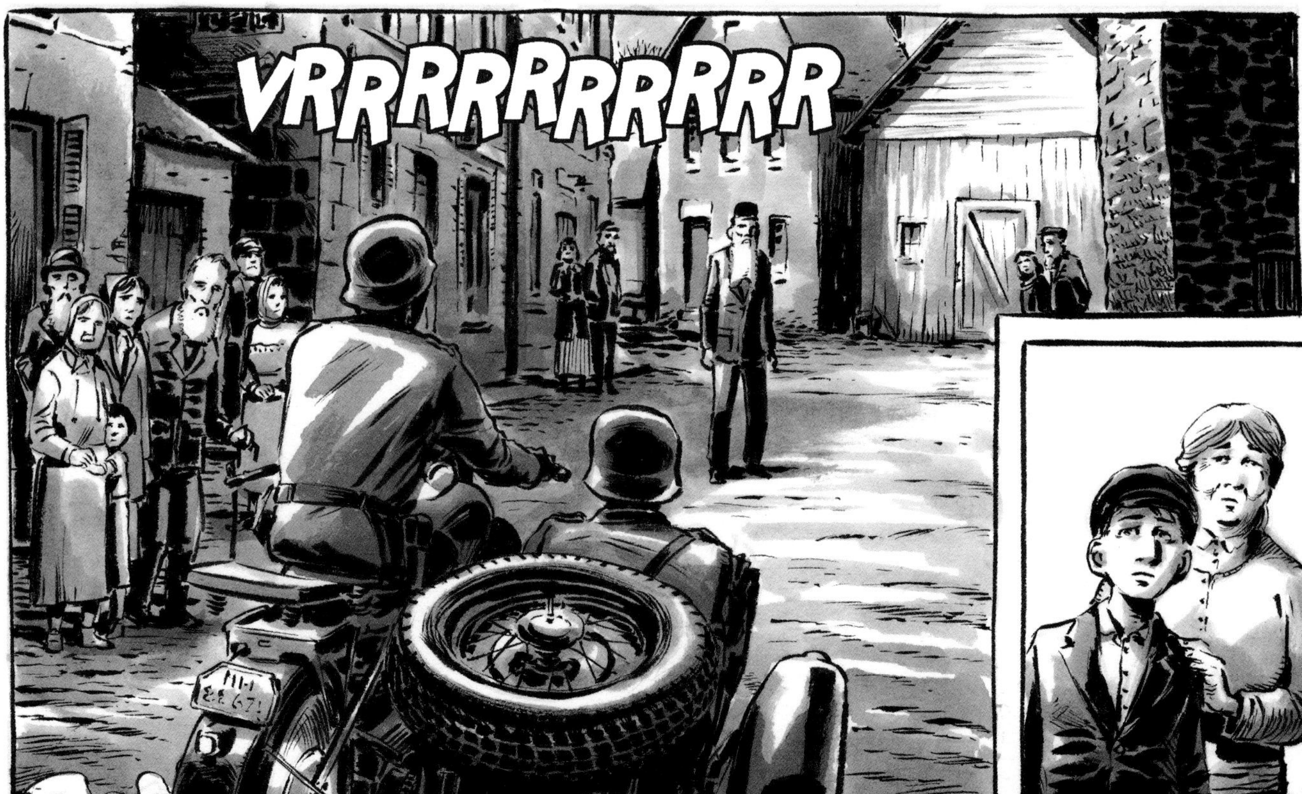
VRRRRRRRRRRR

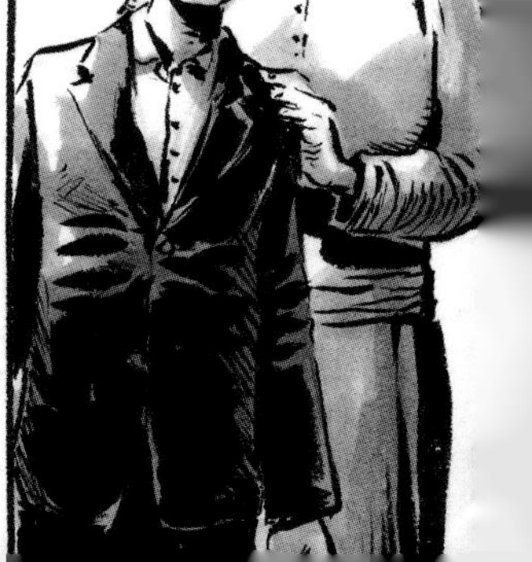

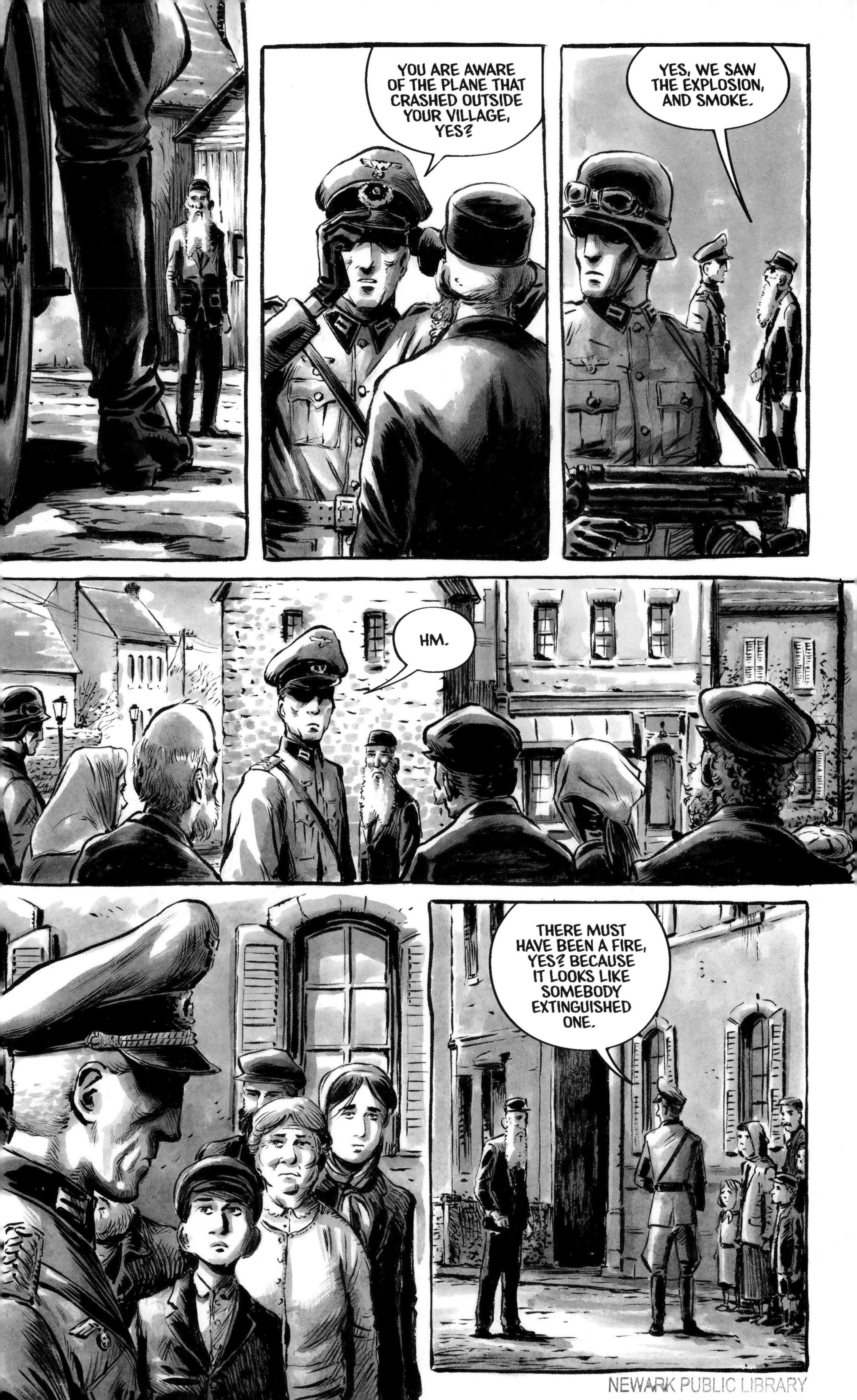
YOU ARE AWARE OF THE PLANE THAT CRASHED OUTSIDE YOUR VILLAGE, YES?
YES, WE SAW THE EXPLOSION, AND SMOKE.
HM.
THERE MUST HAVE BEEN A FIRE, YES? BECAUSE IT LOOKS LIKE SOMEBODY EXTINGUISHED ONE.

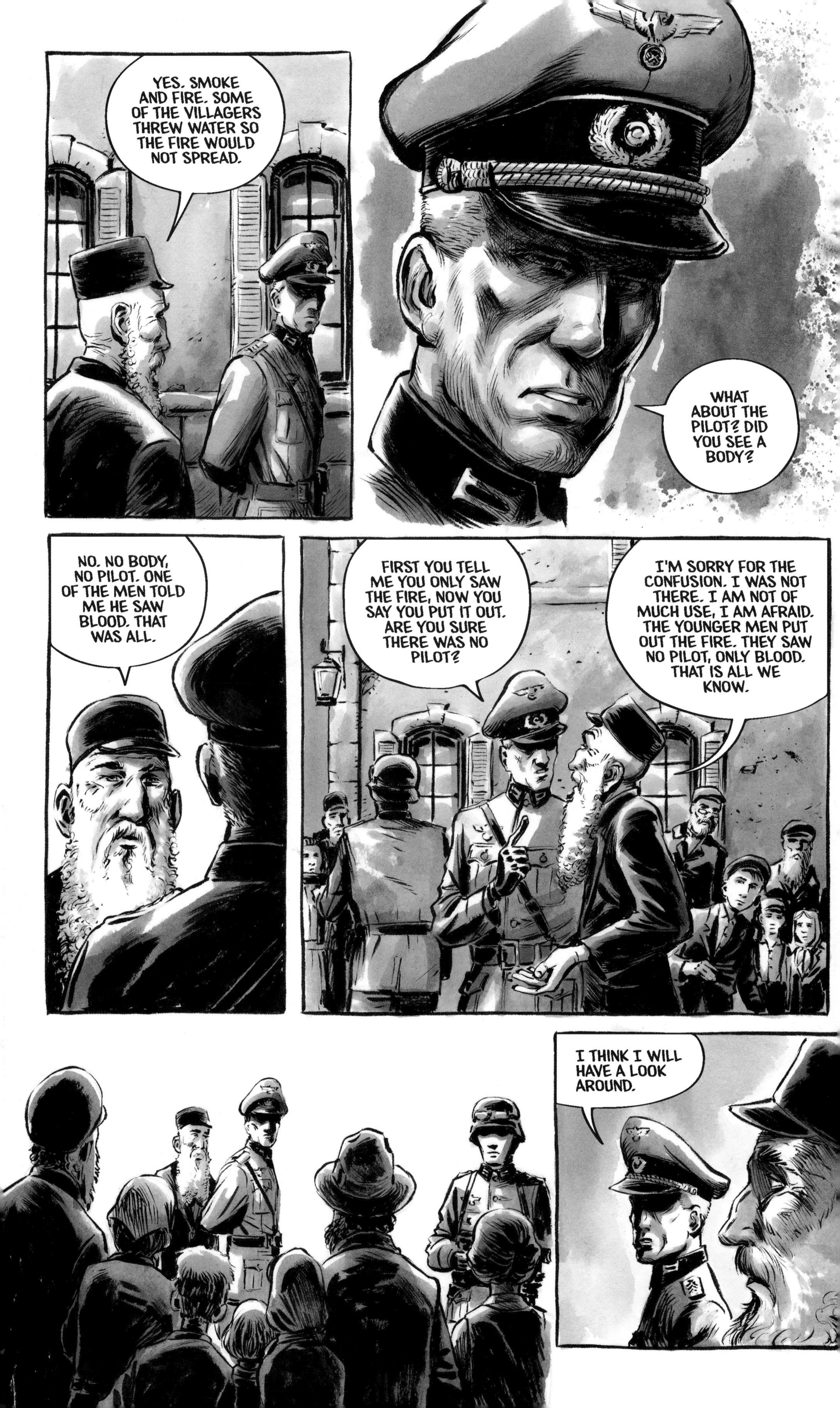
YES. SMOKE AND FIRE. SOME OF THE VILLAGERS THREW WATER SO THE FIRE WOULD NOT SPREAD.
WHAT ABOUT THE PILOT? DID YOU SEE A BODY?
NO. NO BODY, NO PILOT. ONE OF THE MEN TOLD ME HE SAW BLOOD. THAT WAS ALL.
FIRST YOU TELL ME YOU ONLY SAW THE FIRE, NOW YOU SAY YOU PUT IT OUT. ARE YOU SURE THERE WAS NO PILOT?
I'M SORRY FOR THE CONFUSION. I WAS NOT THERE. I AM NOT OF MUCH USE, I AM AFRAID. THE YOUNGER MEN PUT OUT THE FIRE. THEY SAW NO PILOT, ONLY BLOOD. THAT IS ALL WE KNOW.
I THINK I WILL HAVE A LOOK AROUND.

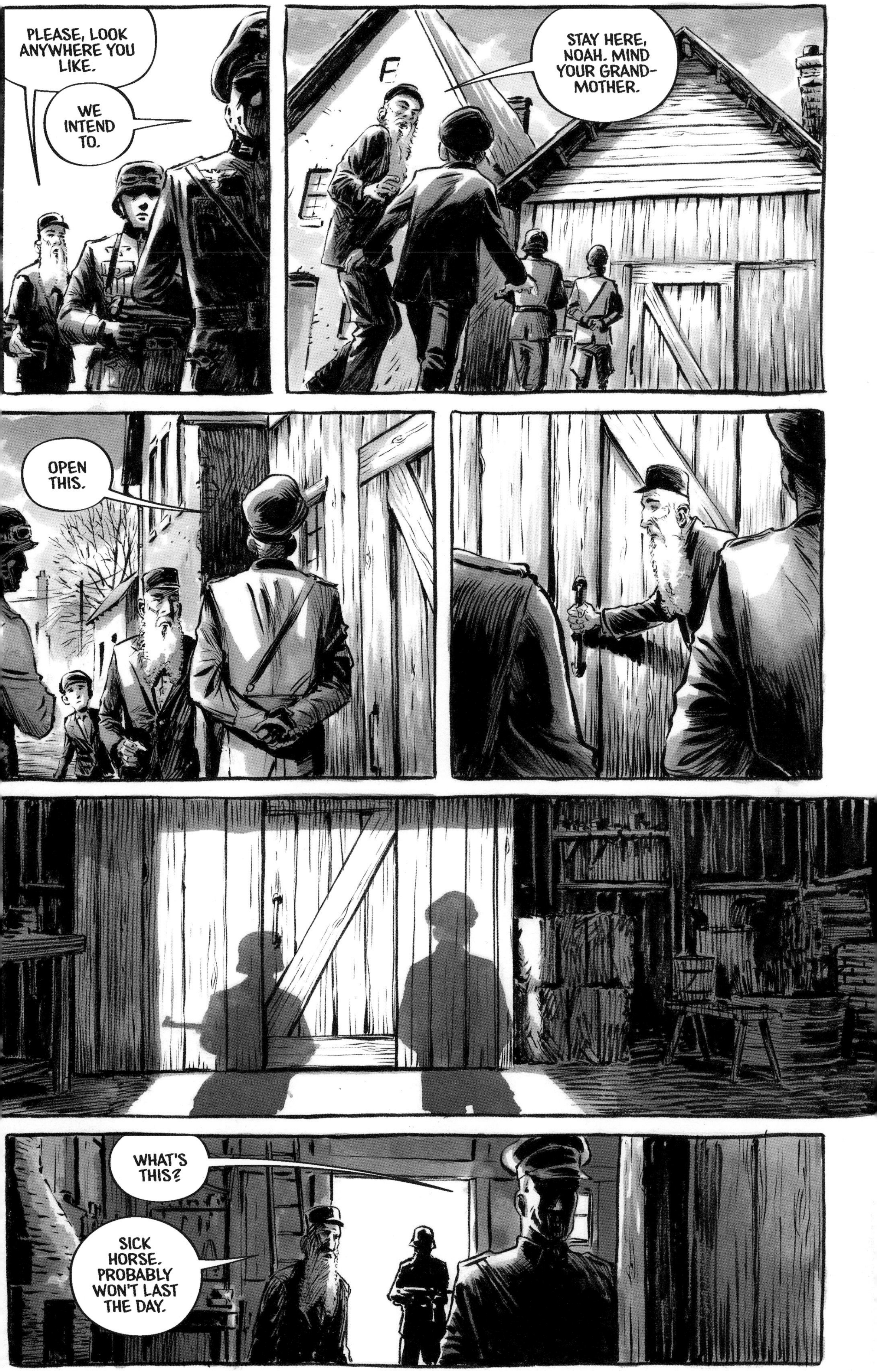
PLEASE, LOOK ANYWHERE YOU LIKE.
WE INTEND TO.
STAY HERE, NOAH. MIND YOUR GRAND-MOTHER.
OPEN THIS.
WHAT'S THIS?
SICK HORSE. PROBABLY WON'T LAST THE DAY.

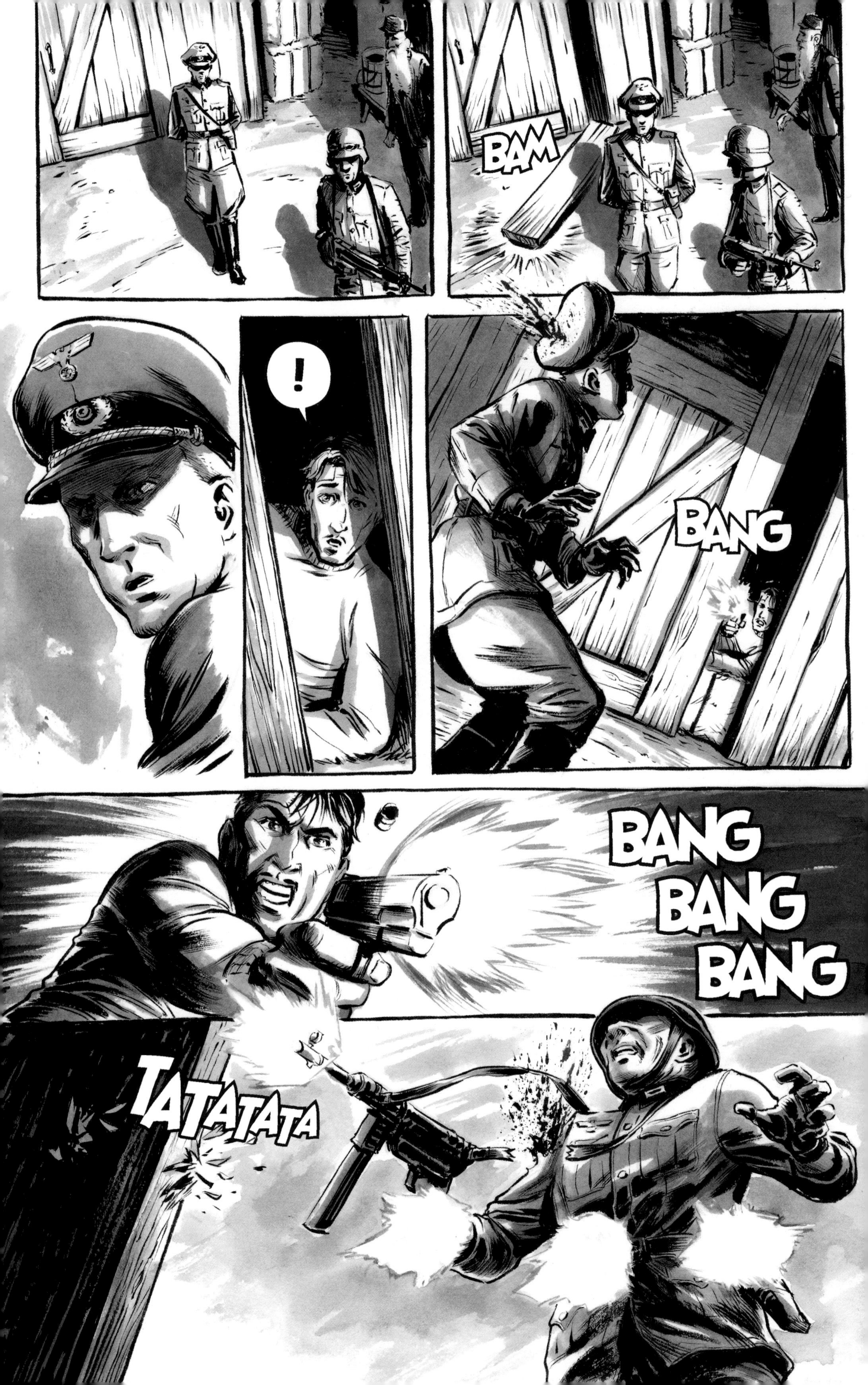
BAM
!
BANG
BANG
BANG
BANG
TATATATA

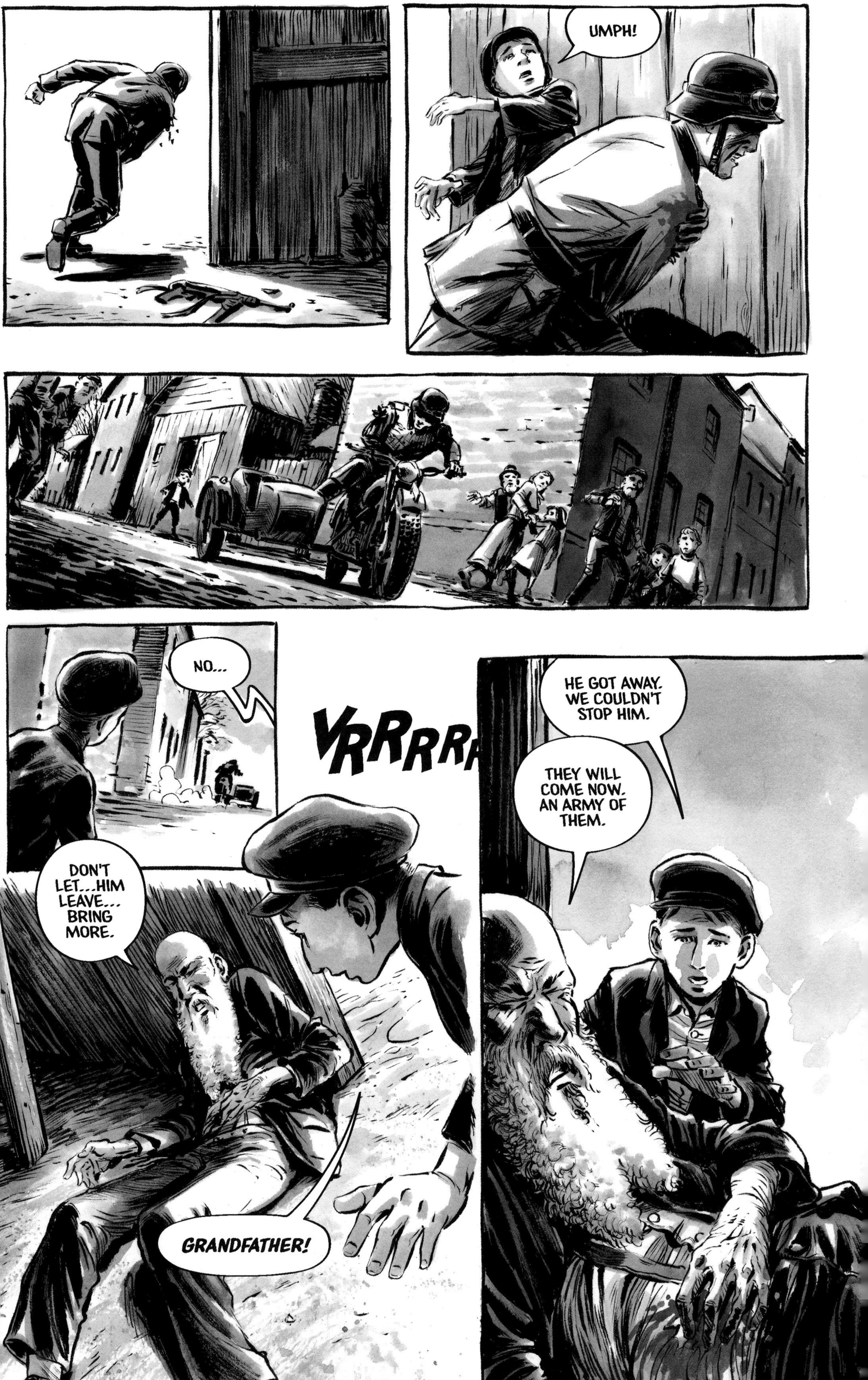
UMPH!
NO...
VRRRRR
HE GOT AWAY. WE COULDN'T STOP HIM.
THEY WILL COME NOW. AN ARMY OF THEM.
DON'T LET...HIM LEAVE... BRING MORE.
GRANDFATHER!

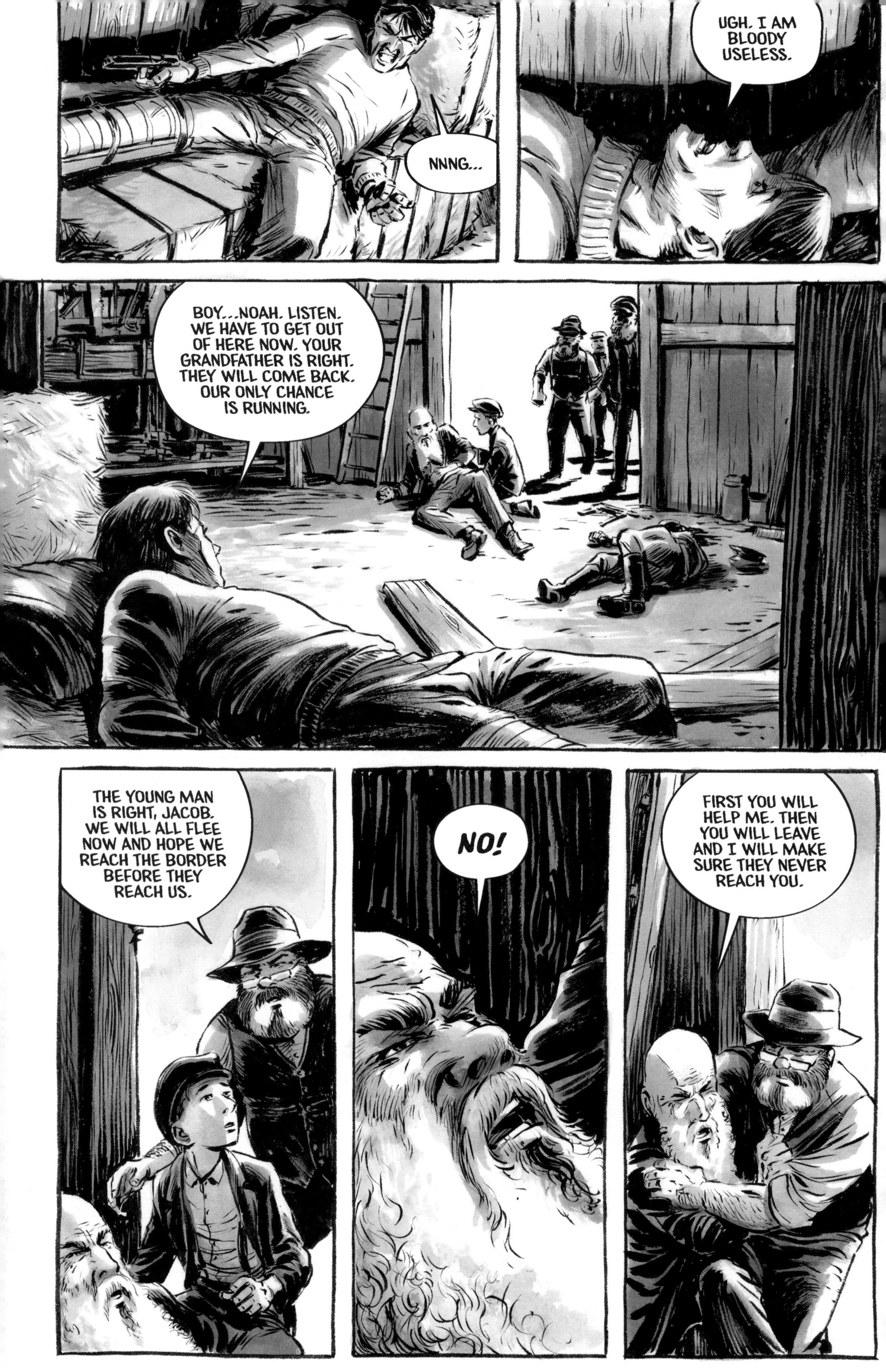
NNNG...
UGH. I AM BLOODY USELESS.
BOY...NOAH. LISTEN. WE HAVE TO GET OUT OF HERE NOW. YOUR GRANDFATHER IS RIGHT. THEY WILL COME BACK. OUR ONLY CHANCE IS RUNNING.
THE YOUNG MAN IS RIGHT, JACOB. WE WILL ALL FLEE NOW AND HOPE WE REACH THE BORDER BEFORE THEY REACH US.
NO!
FIRST YOU WILL HELP ME. THEN YOU WILL LEAVE AND I WILL MAKE SURE THEY NEVER REACH YOU.

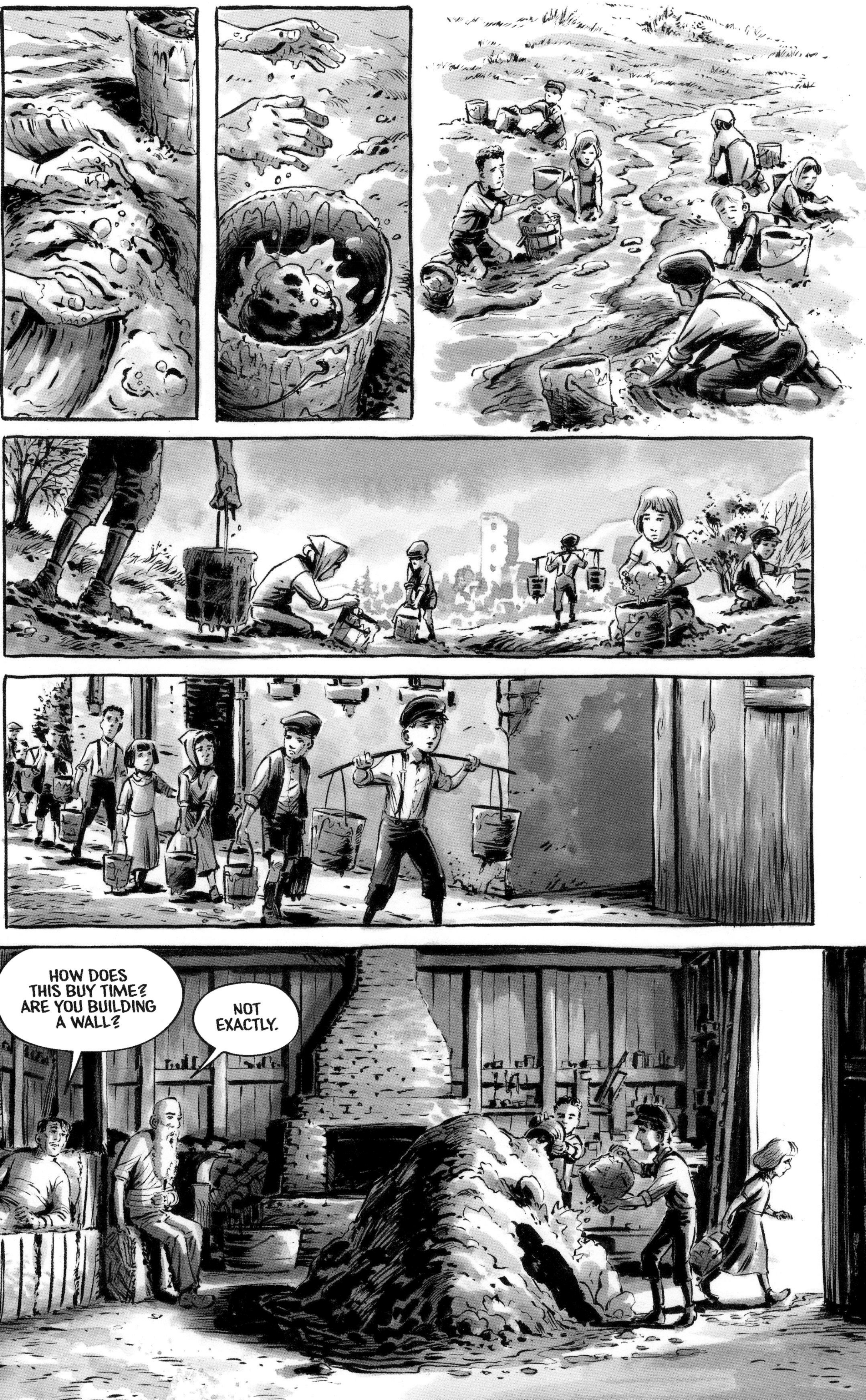
HOW DOES THIS BUY TIME? ARE YOU BUILDING A WALL?
NOT EXACTLY.

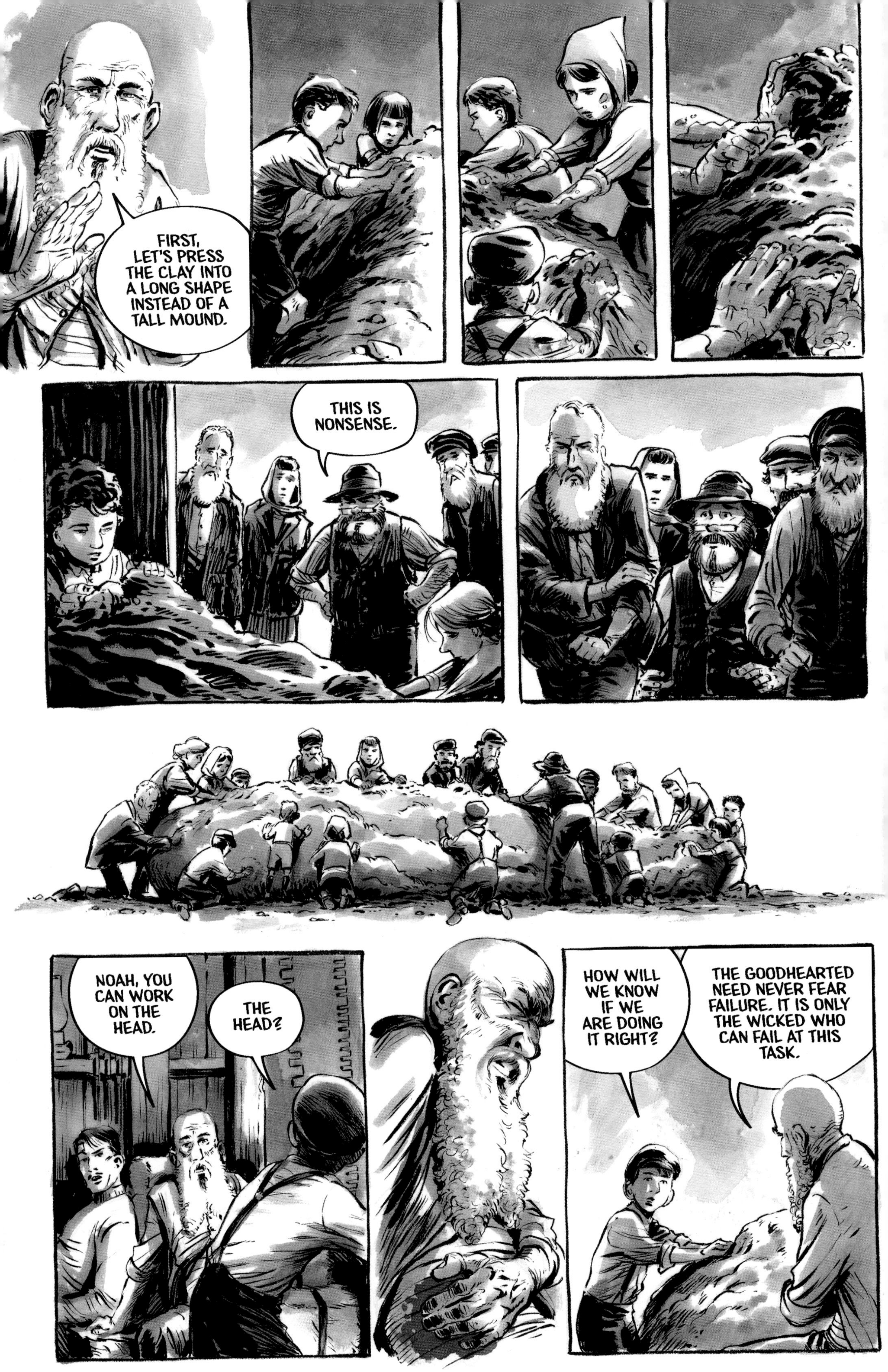
FIRST, LET'S PRESS THE CLAY INTO A LONG SHAPE INSTEAD OF A TALL MOUND.
THIS IS NONSENSE.
NOAH, YOU CAN WORK ON THE HEAD.
THE HEAD?
HOW WILL WE KNOW IF WE ARE DOING IT RIGHT?
THE GOODHEARTED NEED NEVER FEAR FAILURE. IT IS ONLY THE WICKED WHO CAN FAIL AT THIS TASK.

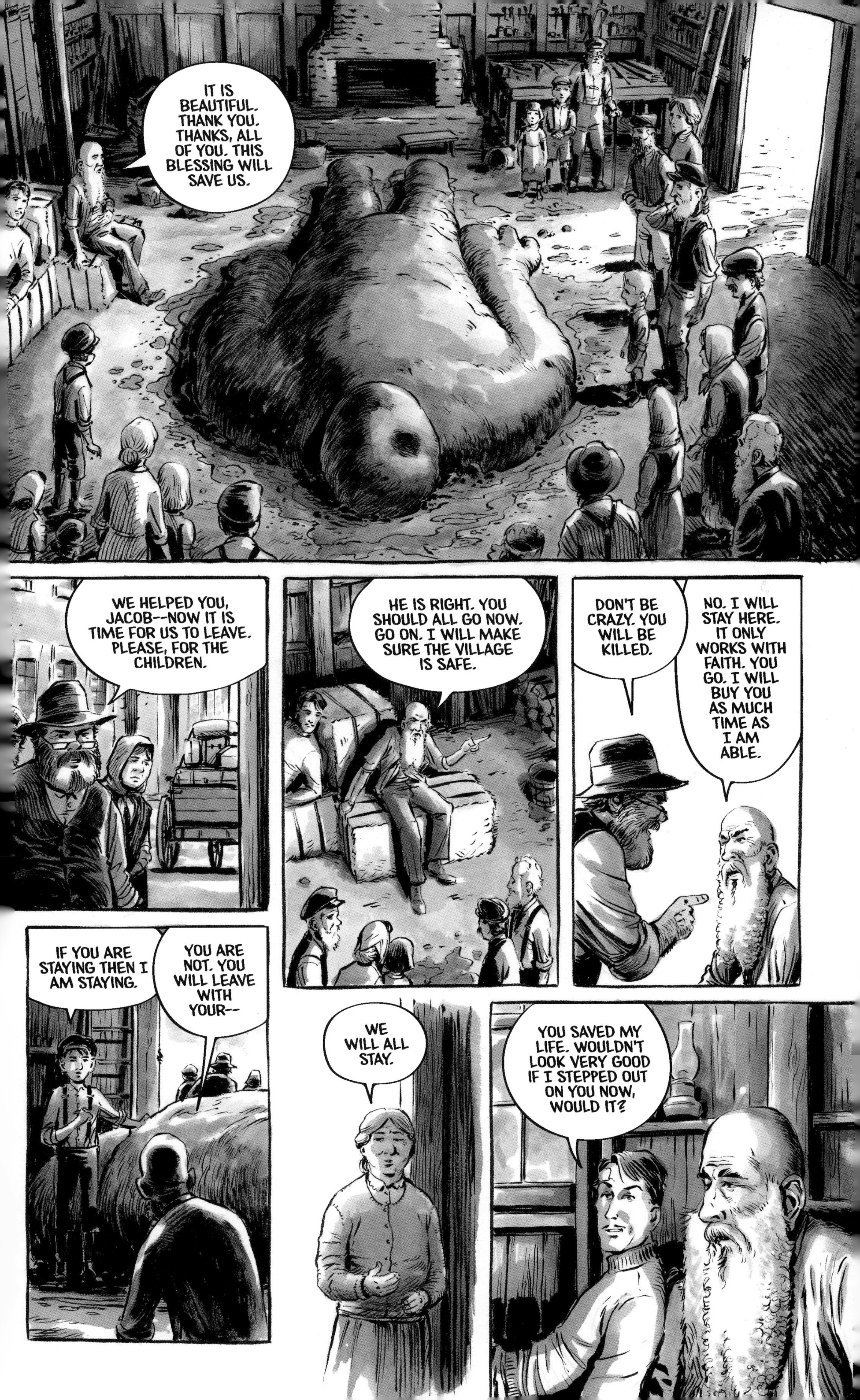
IT IS BEAUTIFUL. THANK YOU. THANKS, ALL OF YOU. THIS BLESSING WILL SAVE US.
WE HELPED YOU, JACOB--NOW IT IS TIME FOR US TO LEAVE. PLEASE, FOR THE CHILDREN.
HE IS RIGHT. YOU SHOULD ALL GO NOW. GO ON. I WILL MAKE SURE THE VILLAGE IS SAFE.
DON'T BE CRAZY. YOU WILL BE KILLED.
NO. I WILL STAY HERE. IT ONLY WORKS WITH FAITH. YOU GO. I WILL BUY YOU AS MUCH TIME AS I AM ABLE.
IF YOU ARE STAYING THEN I AM STAYING.
YOU ARE NOT. YOU WILL LEAVE WITH YOUR--
WE WILL ALL STAY.
YOU SAVED MY LIFE. WOULDN'T LOOK VERY GOOD IF I STEPPED OUT ON YOU NOW, WOULD IT?

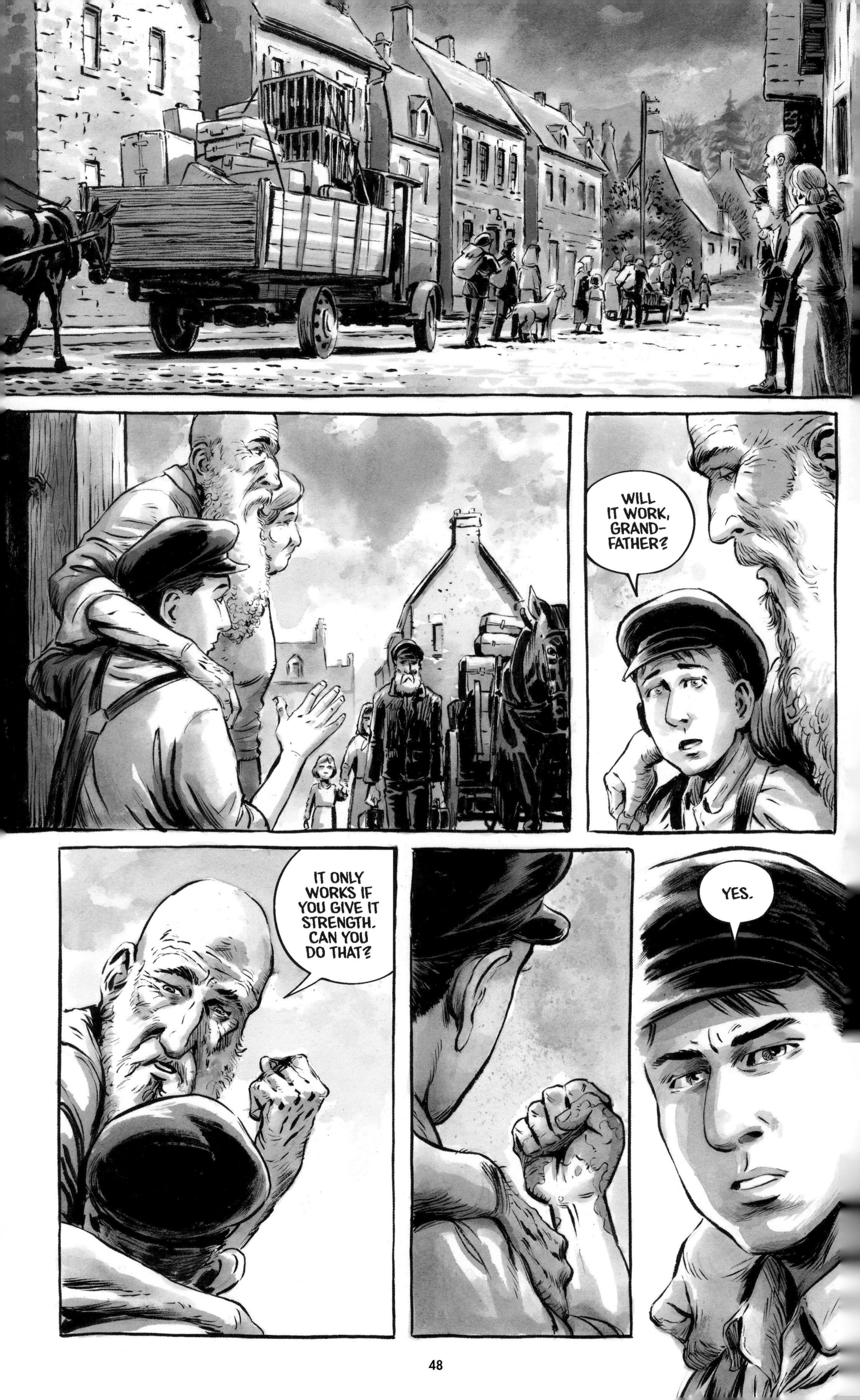
WILL IT WORK, GRAND-FATHER?
IT ONLY WORKS IF YOU GIVE IT STRENGTH. CAN YOU DO THAT?
YES.

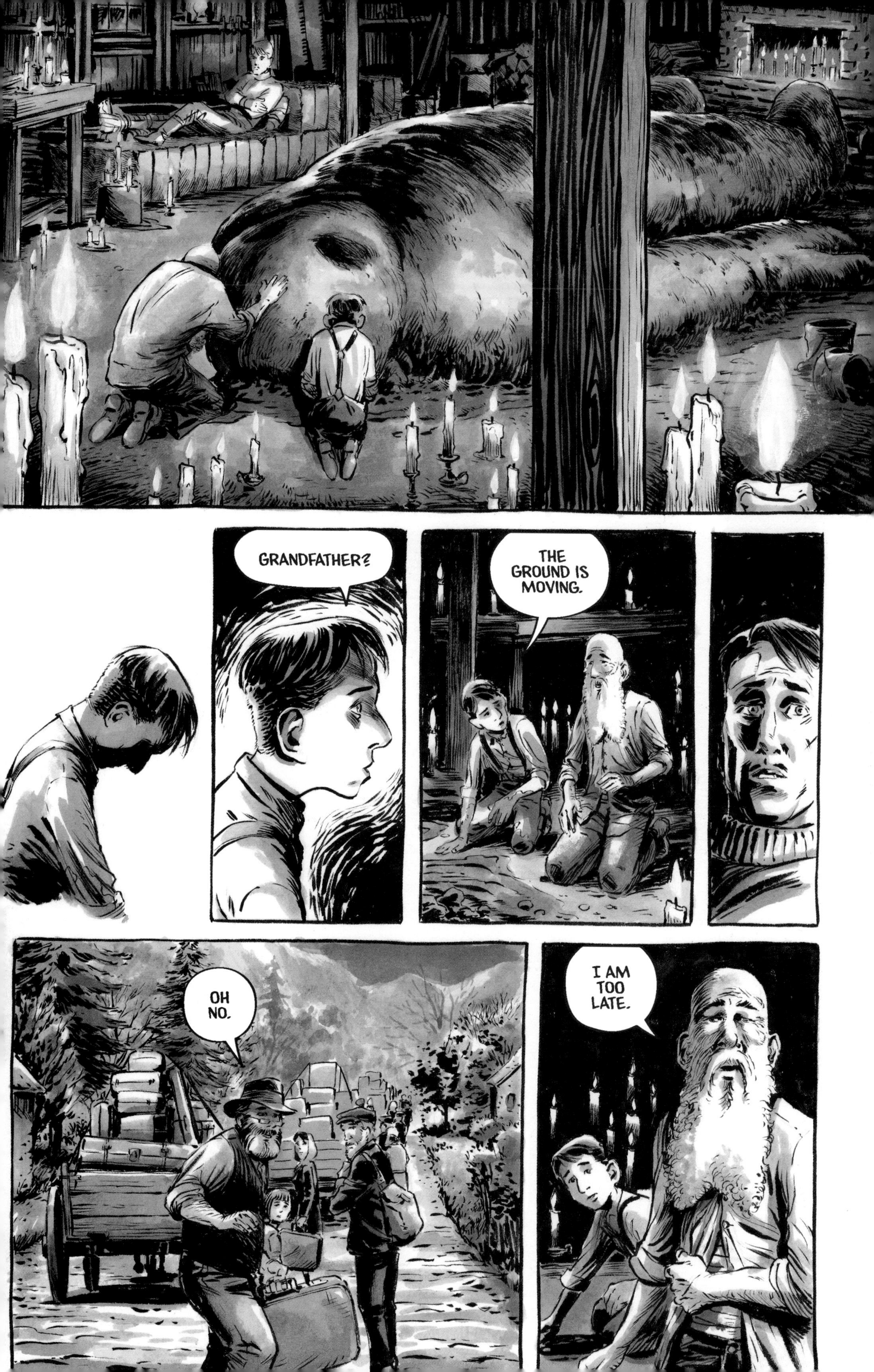
GRANDFATHER?
THE GROUND IS MOVING.
OH NO.
I AM TOO LATE.

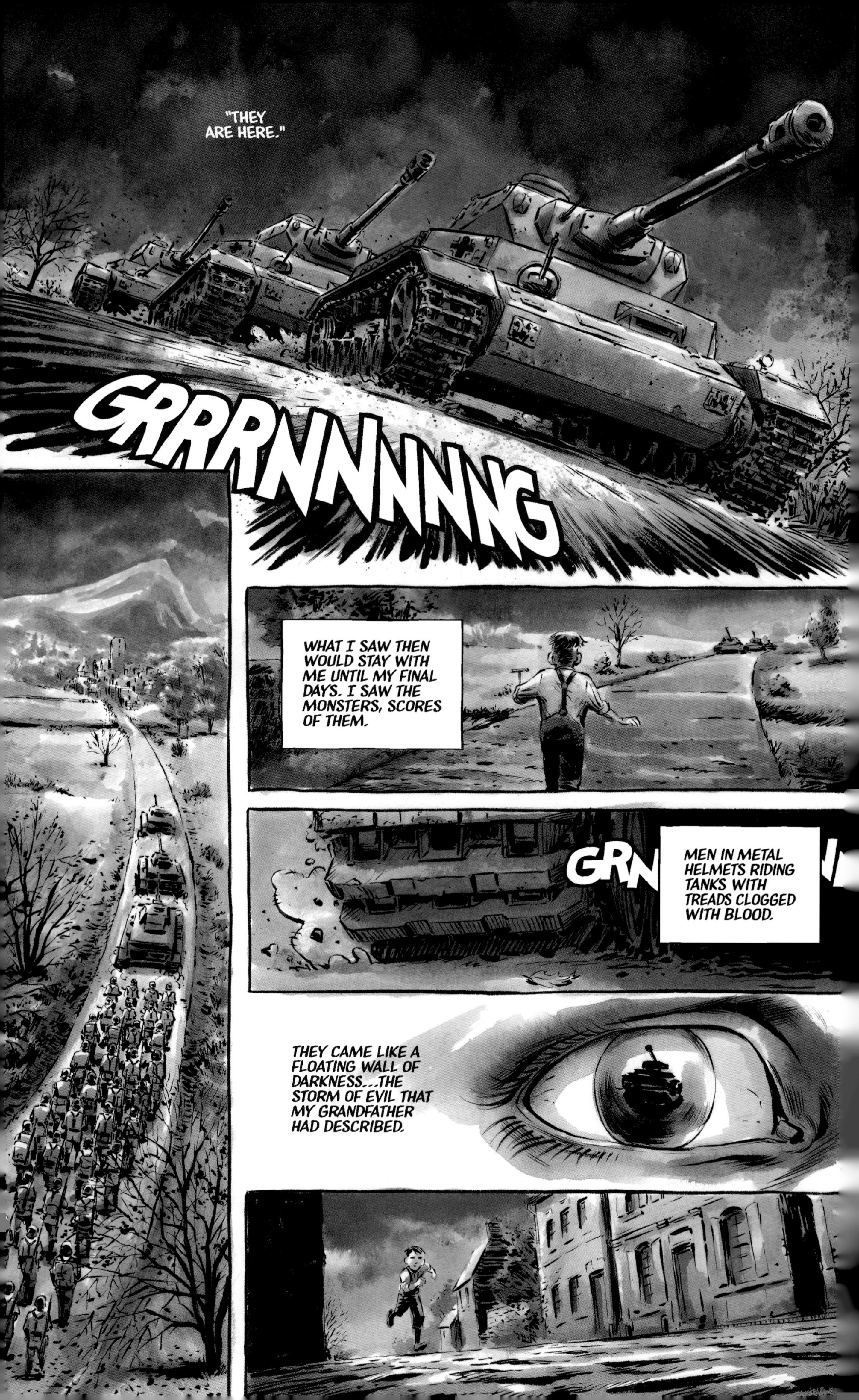
"THEY ARE HERE."
GRRRNNNNNG
WHAT I SAW THEN WOULD STAY WITH ME UNTIL MY FINAL DAYS. I SAW THE MONSTERS, SCORES OF THEM.
GRN
MEN IN METAL HELMETS RIDING TANKS WITH TREADS CLOGGED WITH BLOOD.
THEY CAME LIKE A FLOATING WALL OF DARKNESS...THE STORM OF EVIL THAT MY GRANDFATHER HAD DESCRIBED.

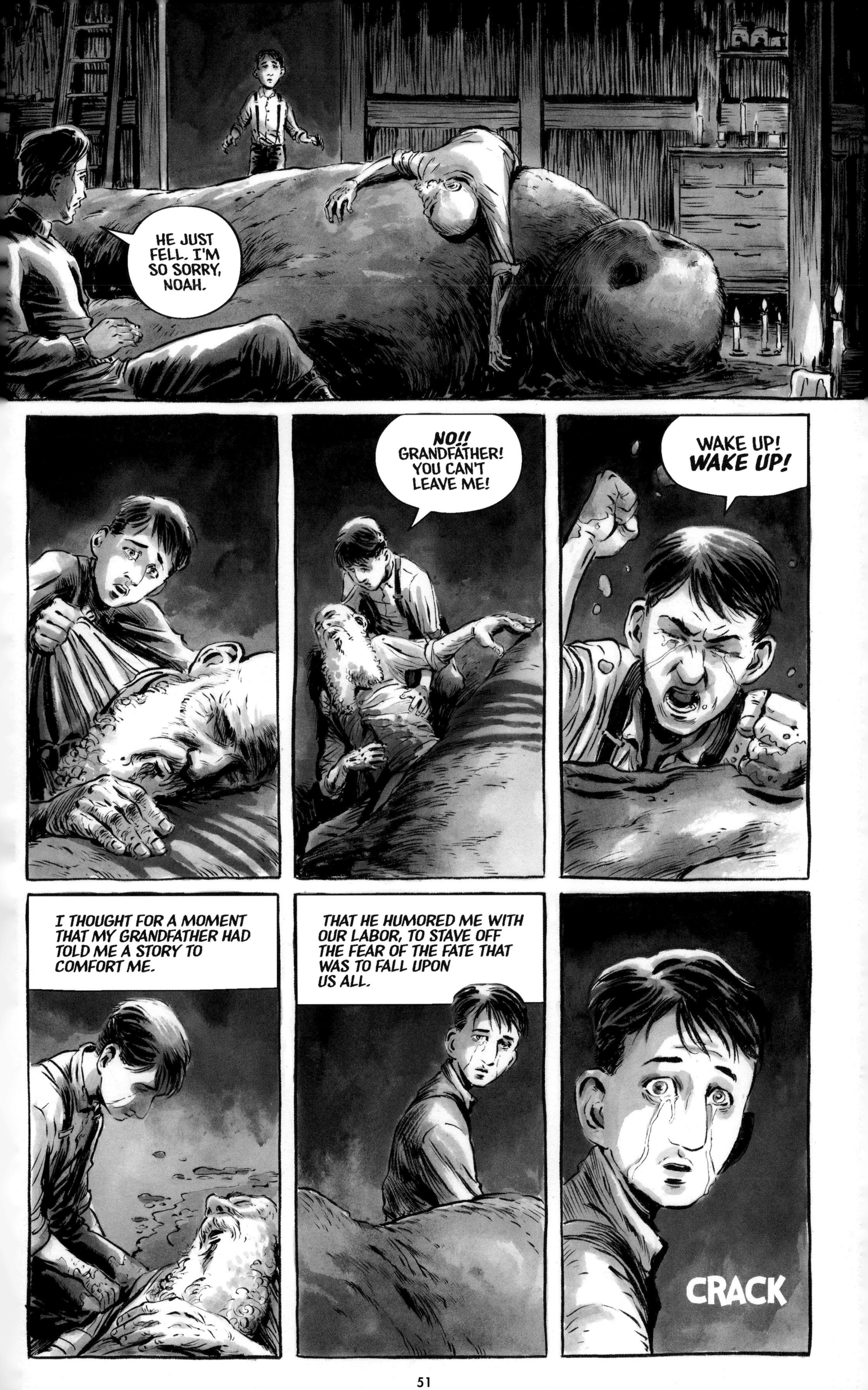
HE JUST FELL. I'M SO SORRY, NOAH.
NO!! GRANDFATHER! YOU CAN'T LEAVE ME!
WAKE UP! WAKE UP!
I THOUGHT FOR A MOMENT THAT MY GRANDFATHER HAD TOLD ME A STORY TO COMFORT ME.
THAT HE HUMORED ME WITH OUR LABOR, TO STAVE OFF THE FEAR OF THE FATE THAT WAS TO FALL UPON US ALL.
CRACK

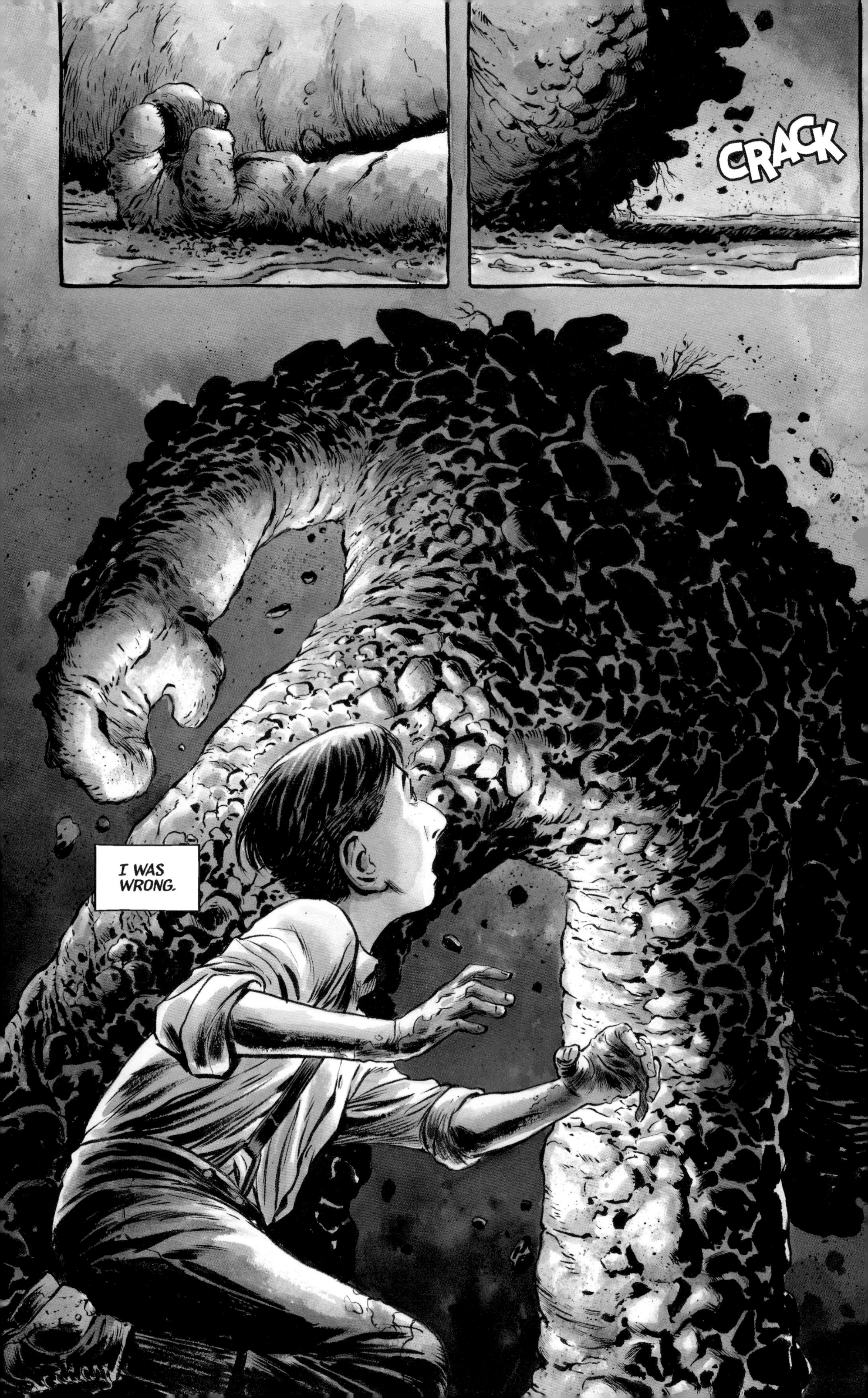
CRACK
I WAS WRONG.

CHAPTER THREE

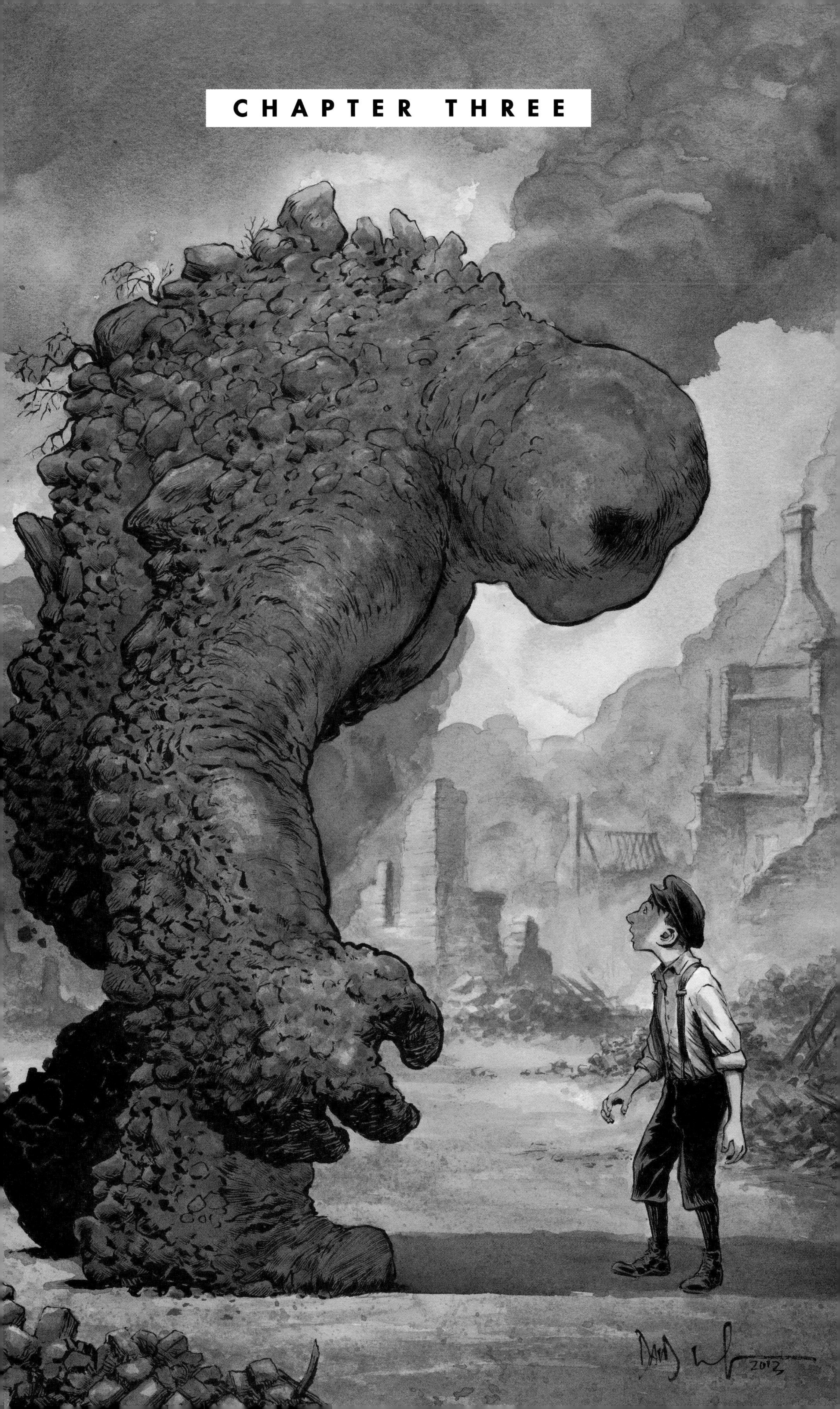

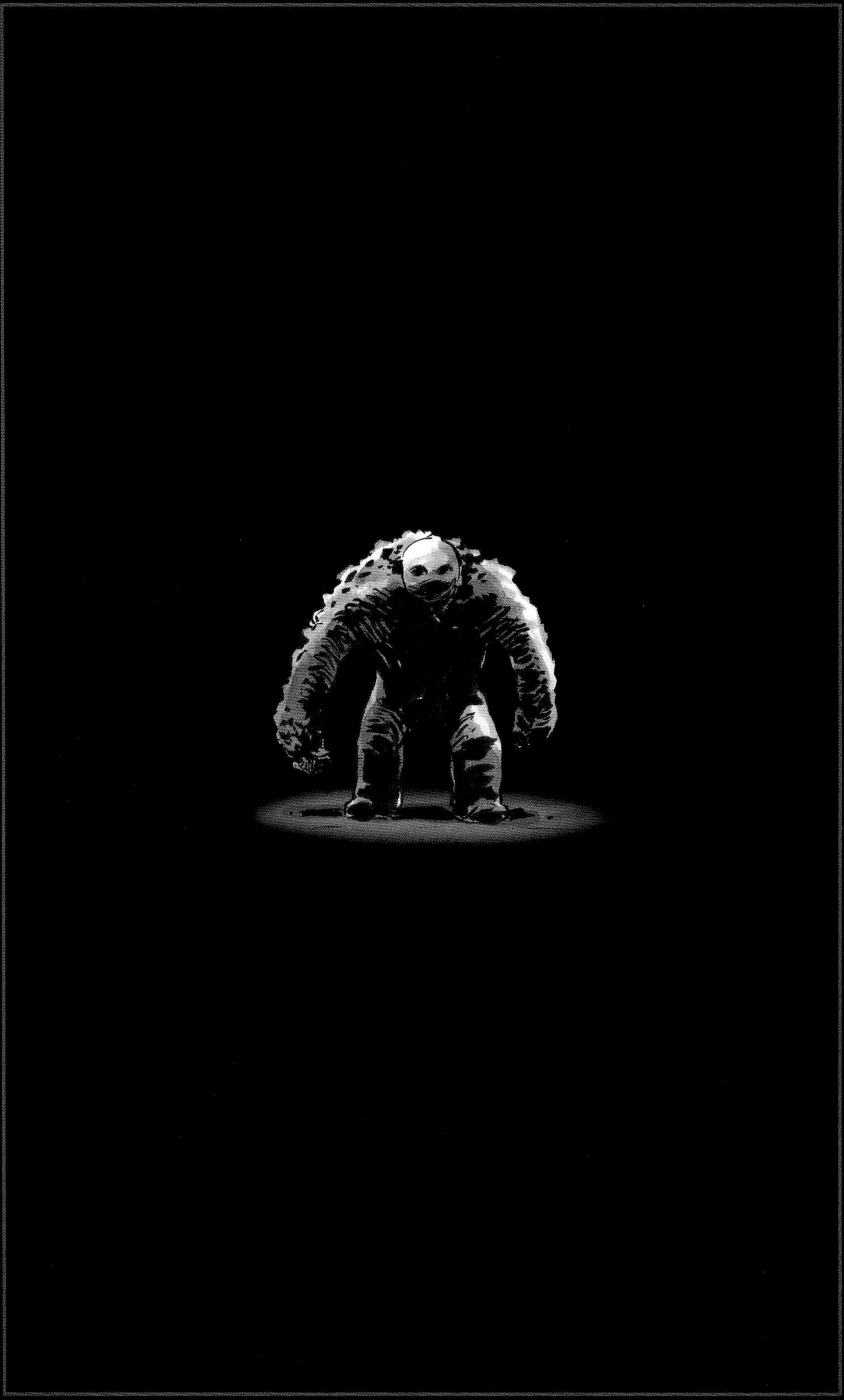

GRANDFATHER WAS RIGHT. HE'S GOING TO HELP US.

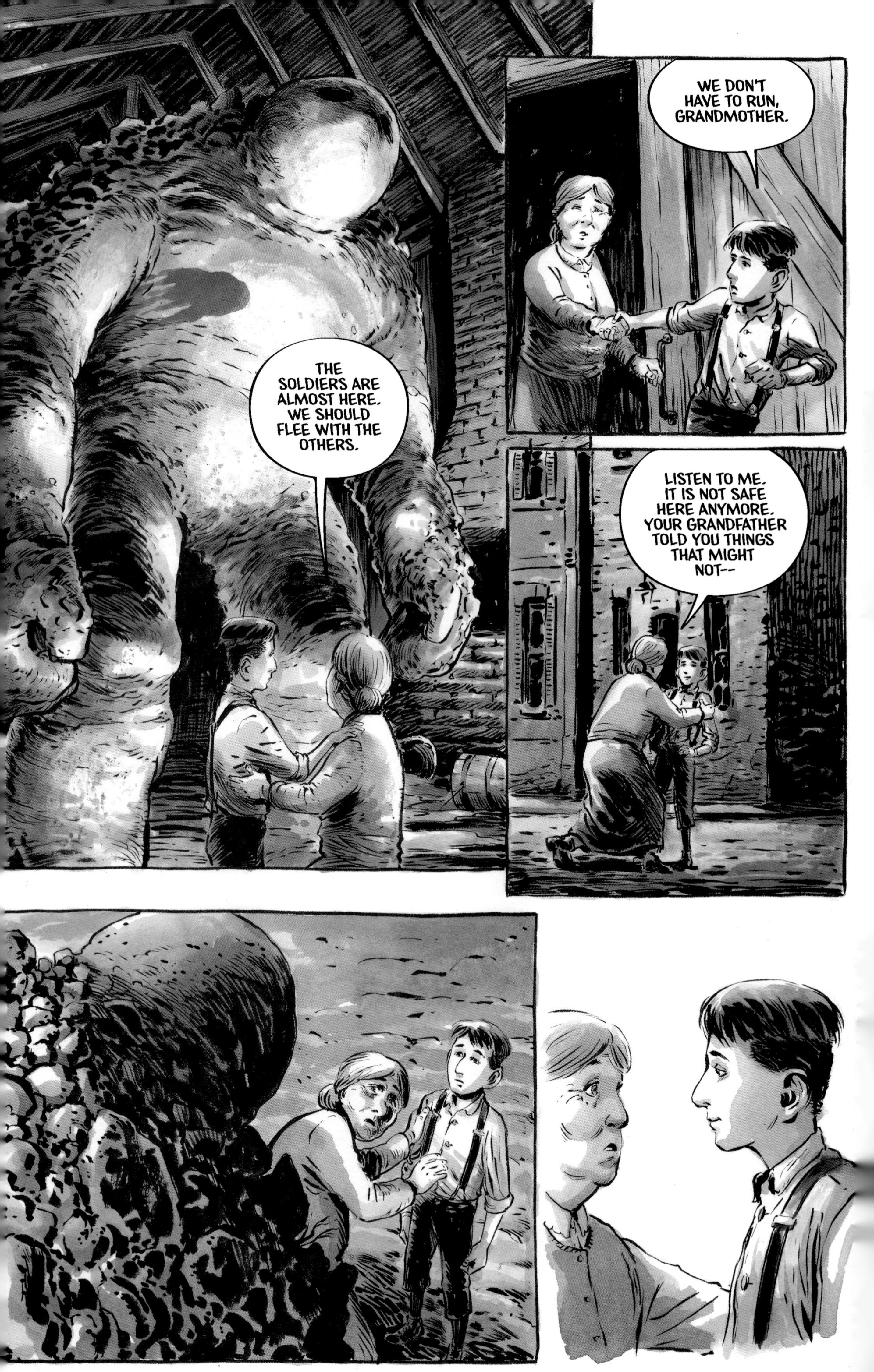
WE DON'T HAVE TO RUN, GRANDMOTHER.
THE SOLDIERS ARE ALMOST HERE. WE SHOULD FLEE WITH THE OTHERS.
LISTEN TO ME. IT IS NOT SAFE HERE ANYMORE. YOUR GRANDFATHER TOLD YOU THINGS THAT MIGHT NOT--

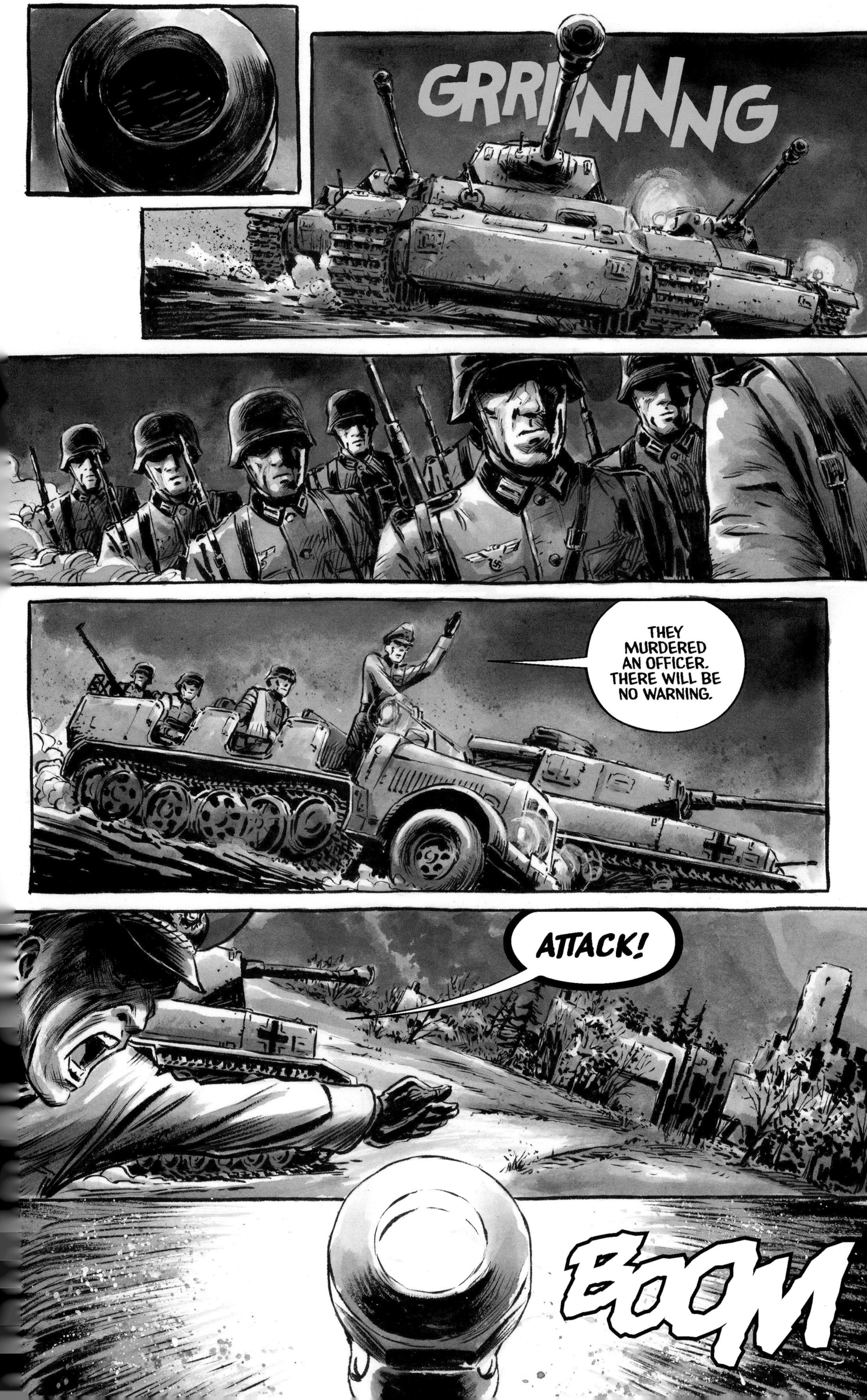
GRRRNNNG
THEY MURDERED AN OFFICER. THERE WILL BE NO WARNING.
ATTACK!
BOOM

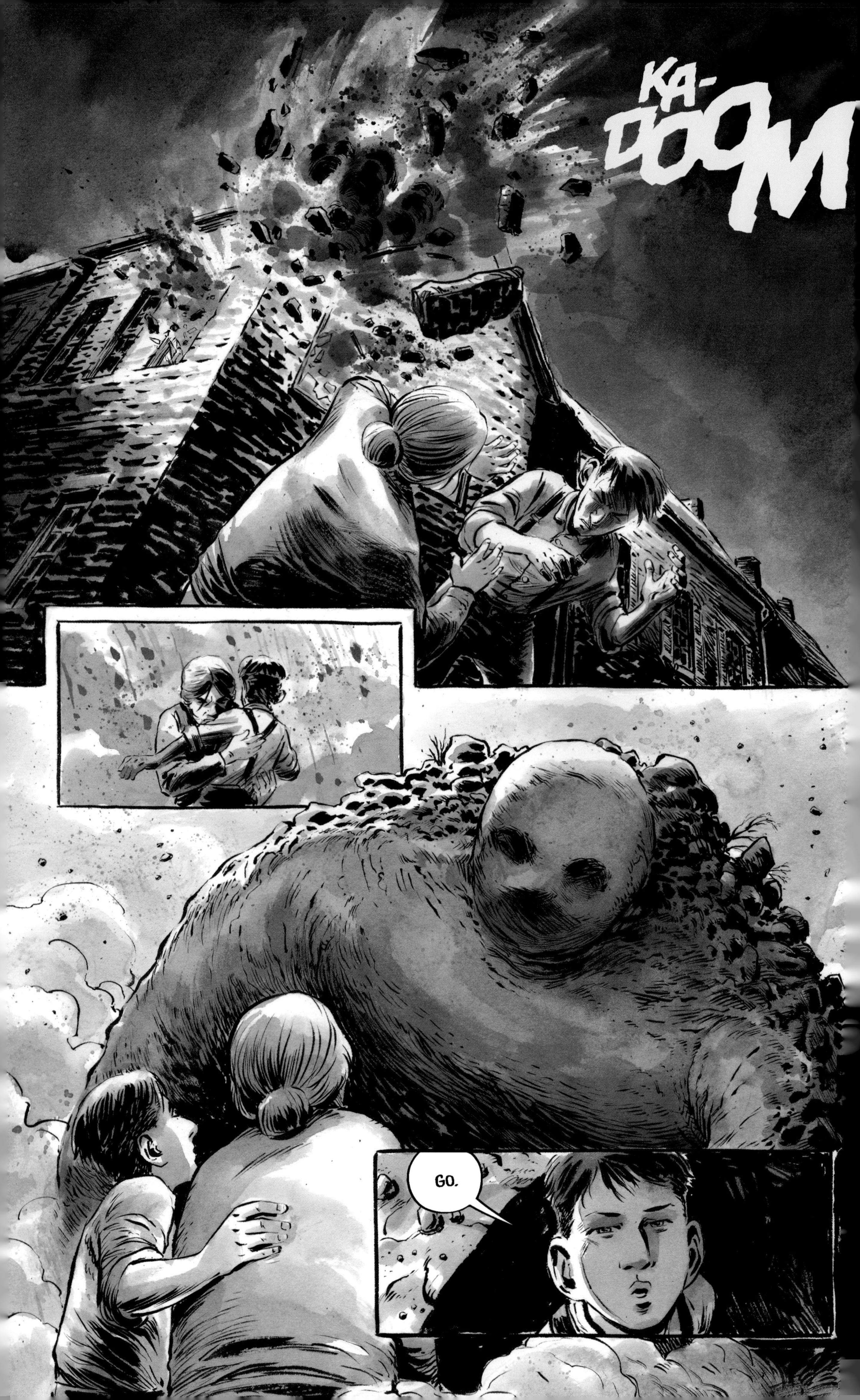
KA-DOOM
GO.

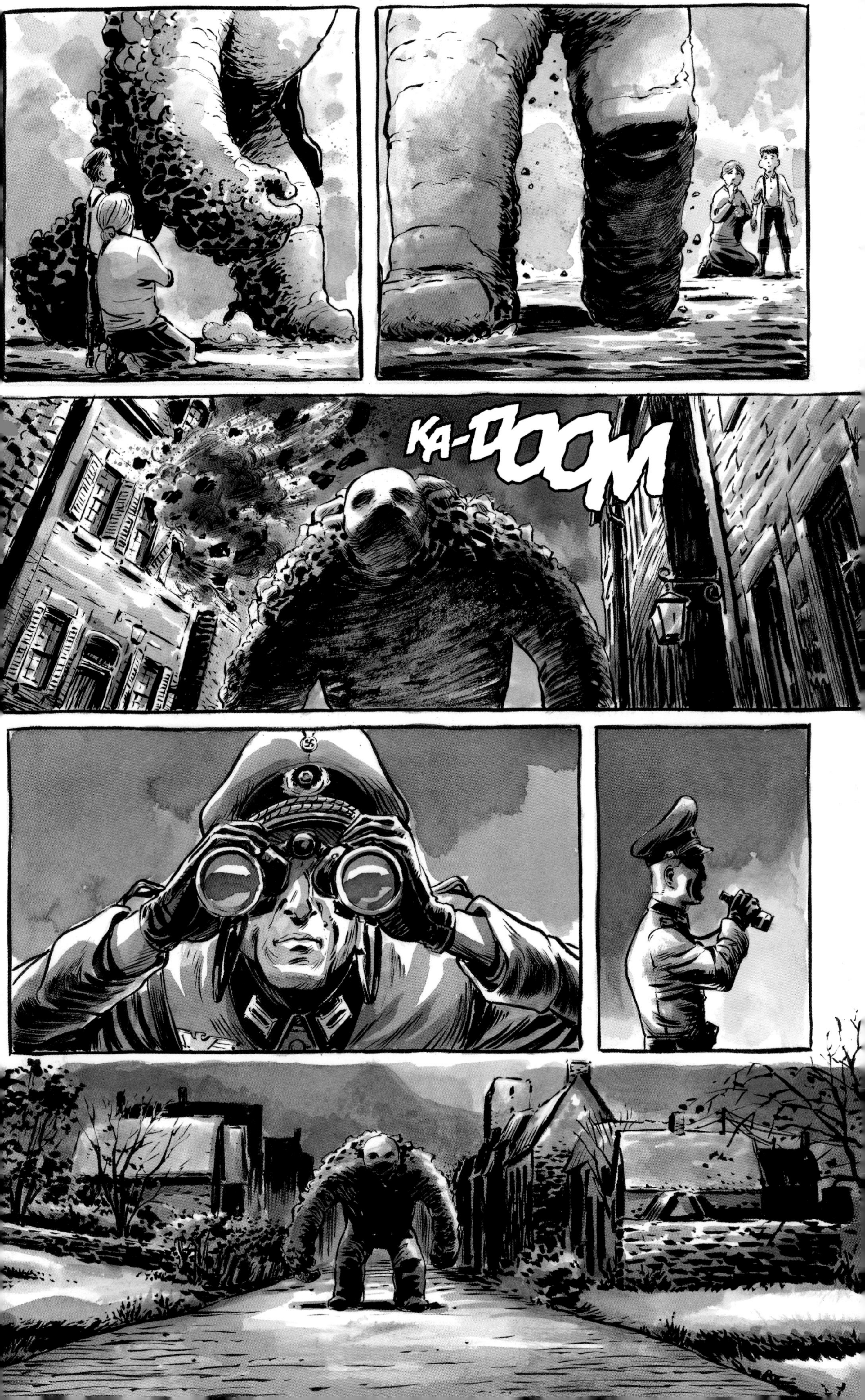
KA-DOOM

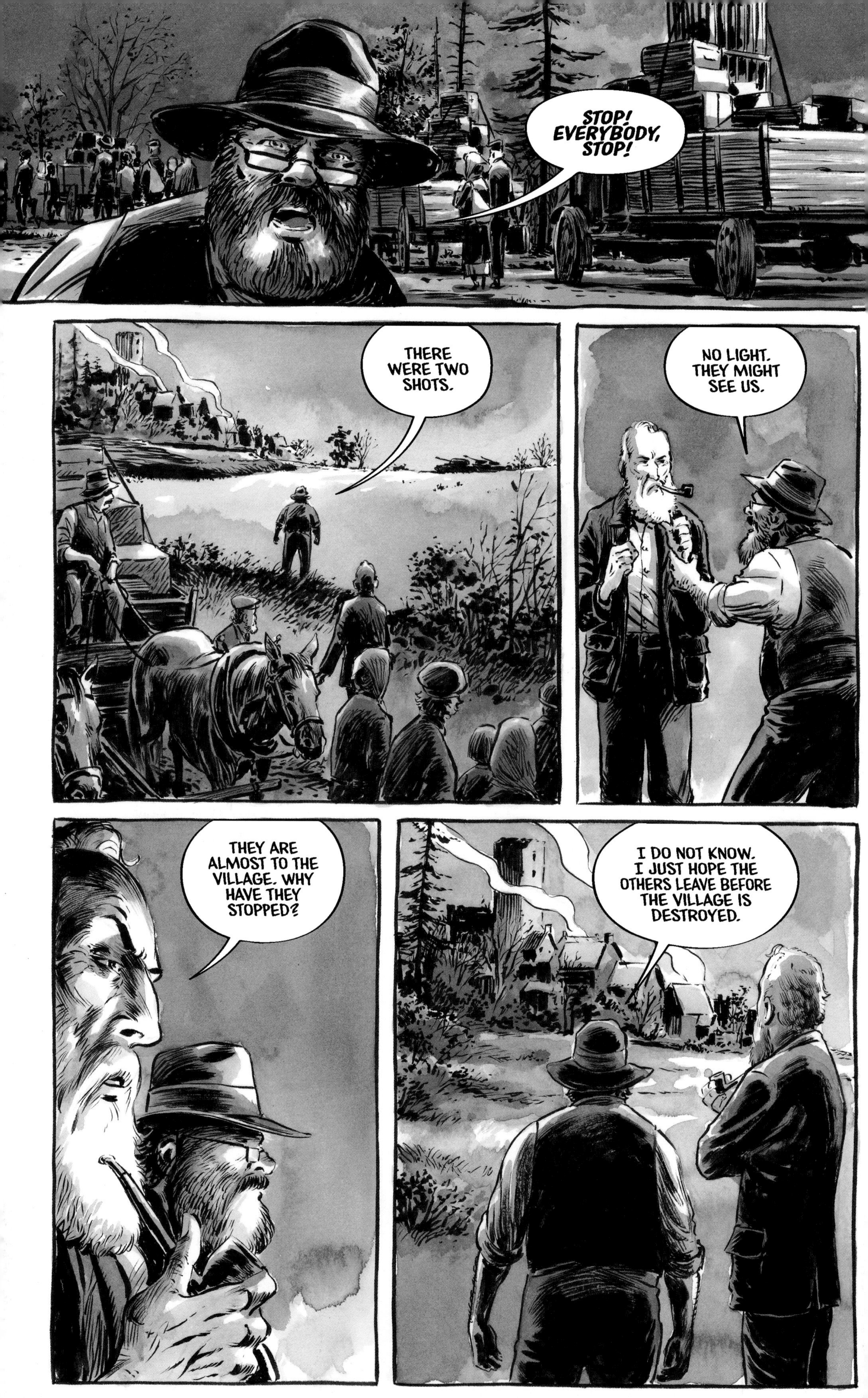
STOP! EVERYBODY, STOP!
THERE WERE TWO SHOTS.
NO LIGHT. THEY MIGHT SEE US.
THEY ARE ALMOST TO THE VILLAGE. WHY HAVE THEY STOPPED?
I DO NOT KNOW. I JUST HOPE THE OTHERS LEAVE BEFORE THE VILLAGE IS DESTROYED.

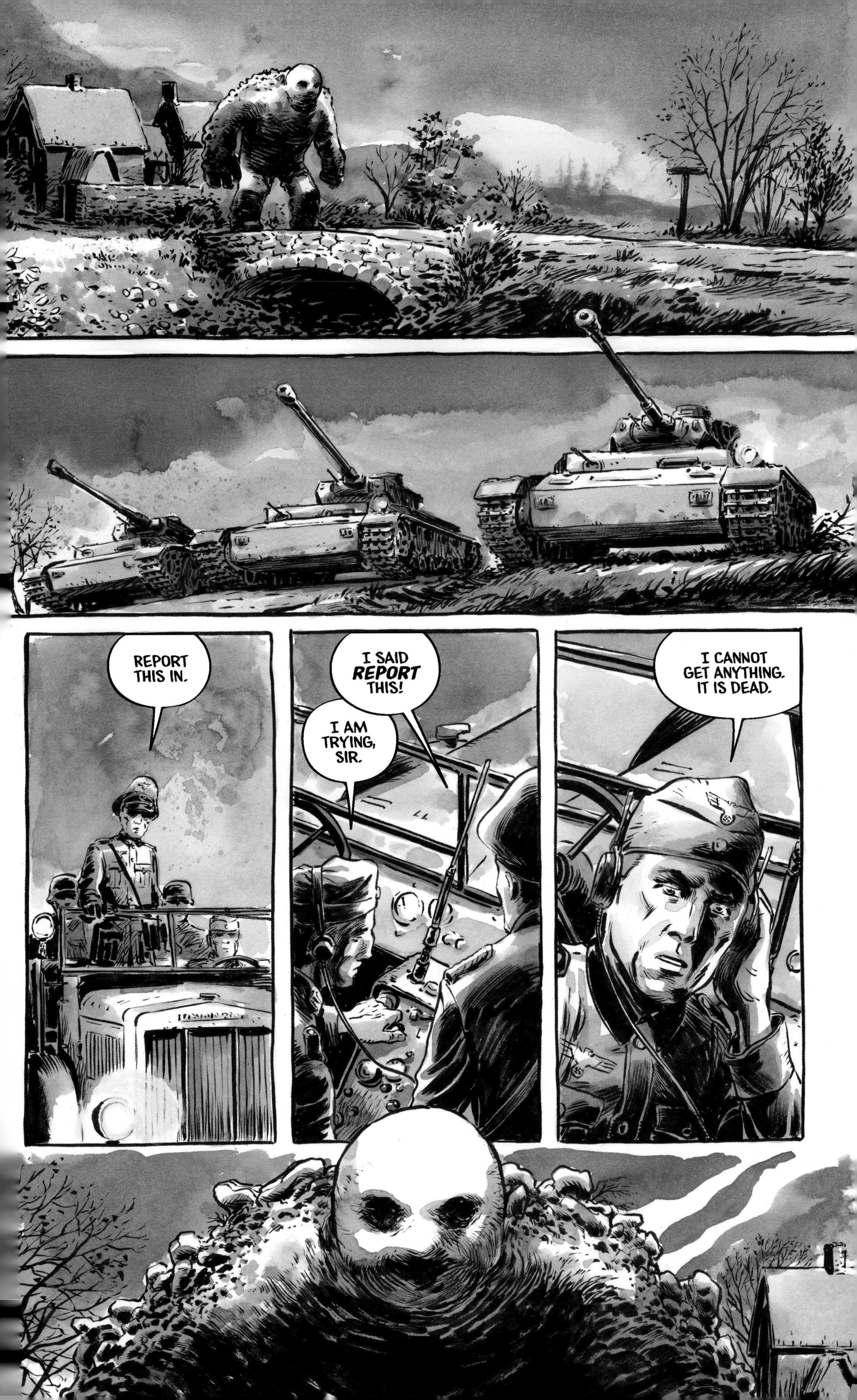
REPORT THIS IN.
I SAID REPORT THIS!
I AM TRYING, SIR.
I CANNOT GET ANYTHING. IT IS DEAD.

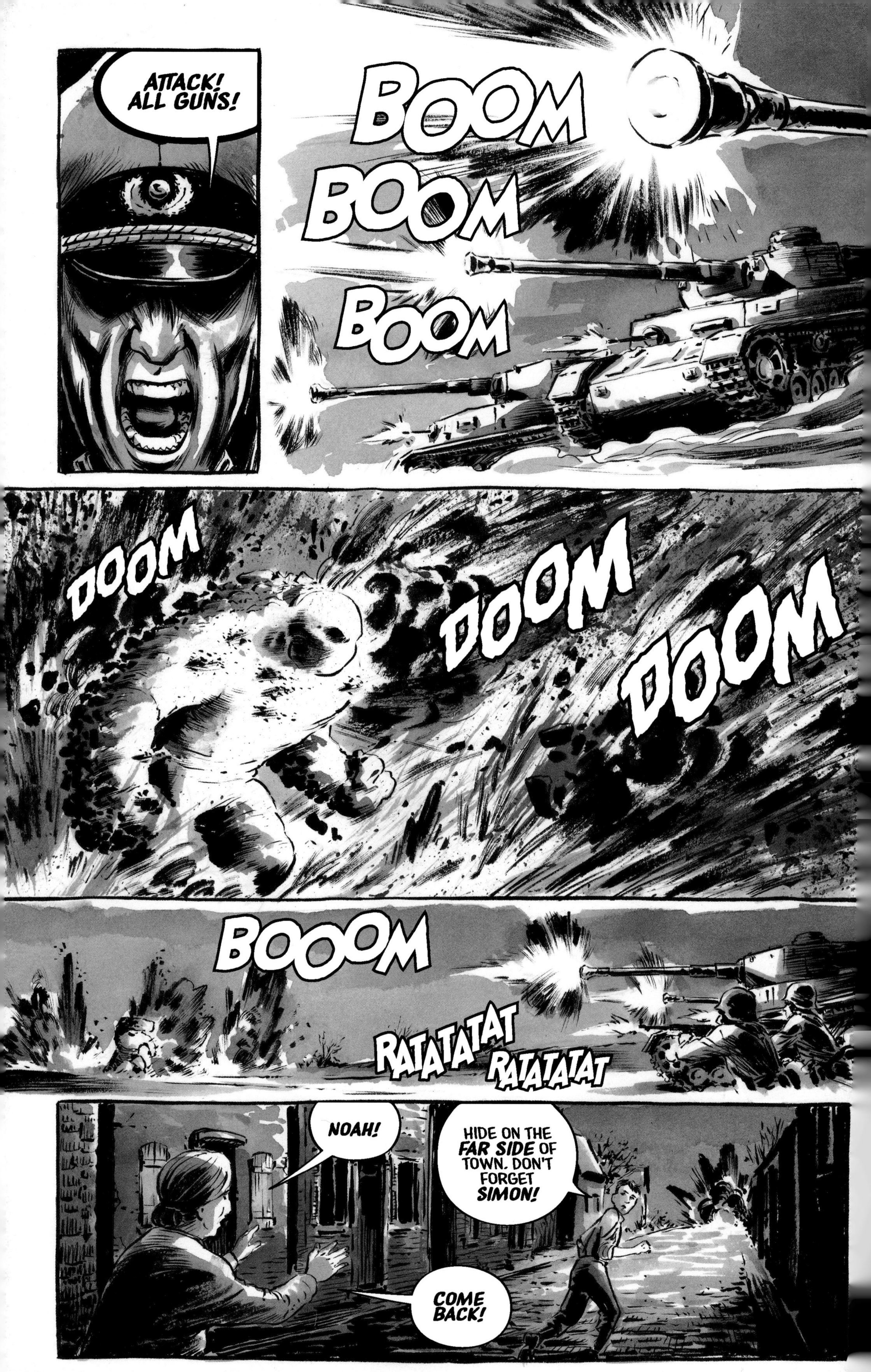

ATTACK! ALL GUNS!
BOOM
BOOM
BOOM
DOOM
DOOM
DOOM
BOOOM
RATATATAT
RATATATAT
NOAH!
HIDE ON THE FAR SIDE OF TOWN. DON'T FORGET SIMON!
COME BACK!

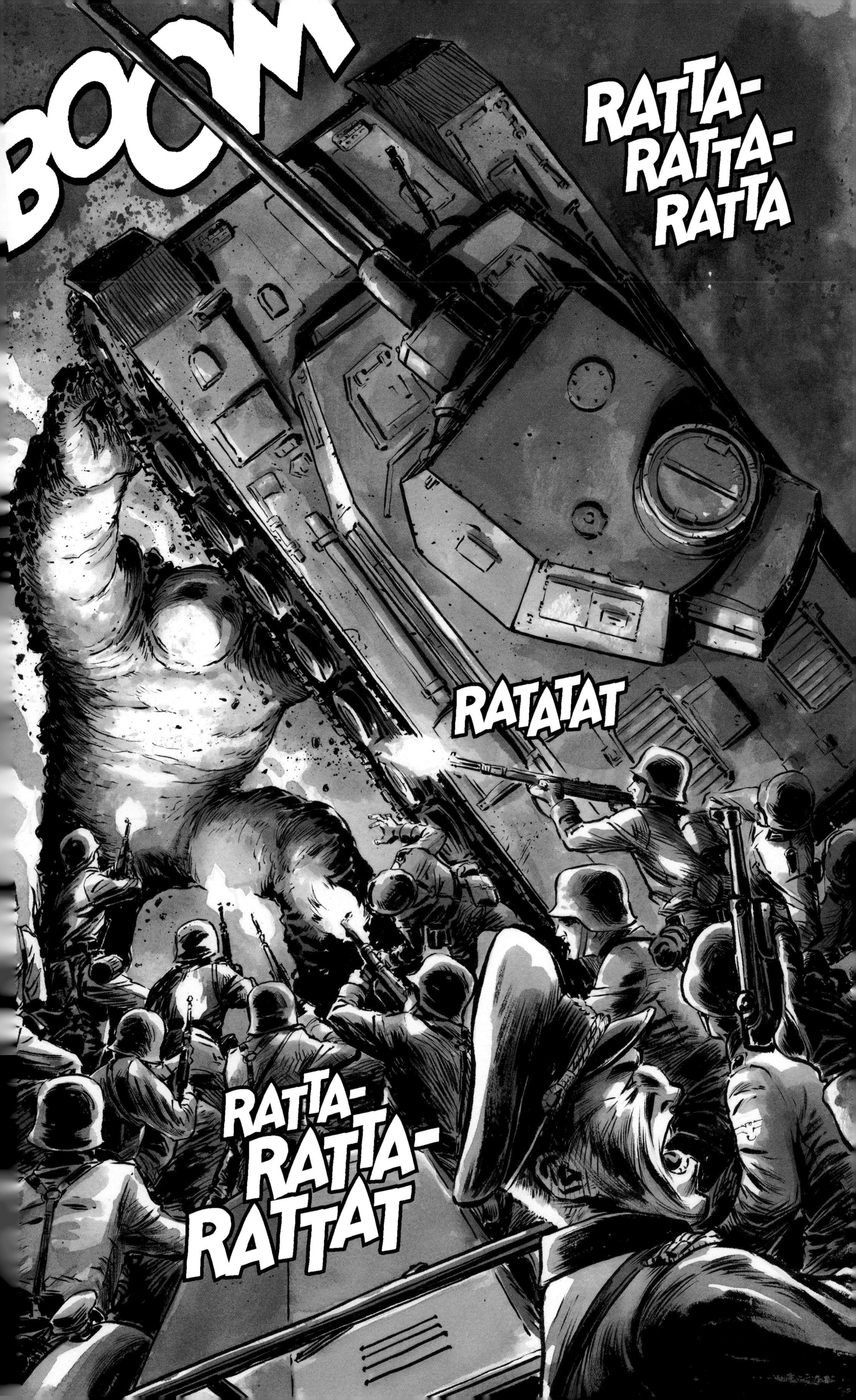
BOOM
RATTA-
RATTA-
RATTA
RATATAT
RATTA-
RATTA-
RATTAT

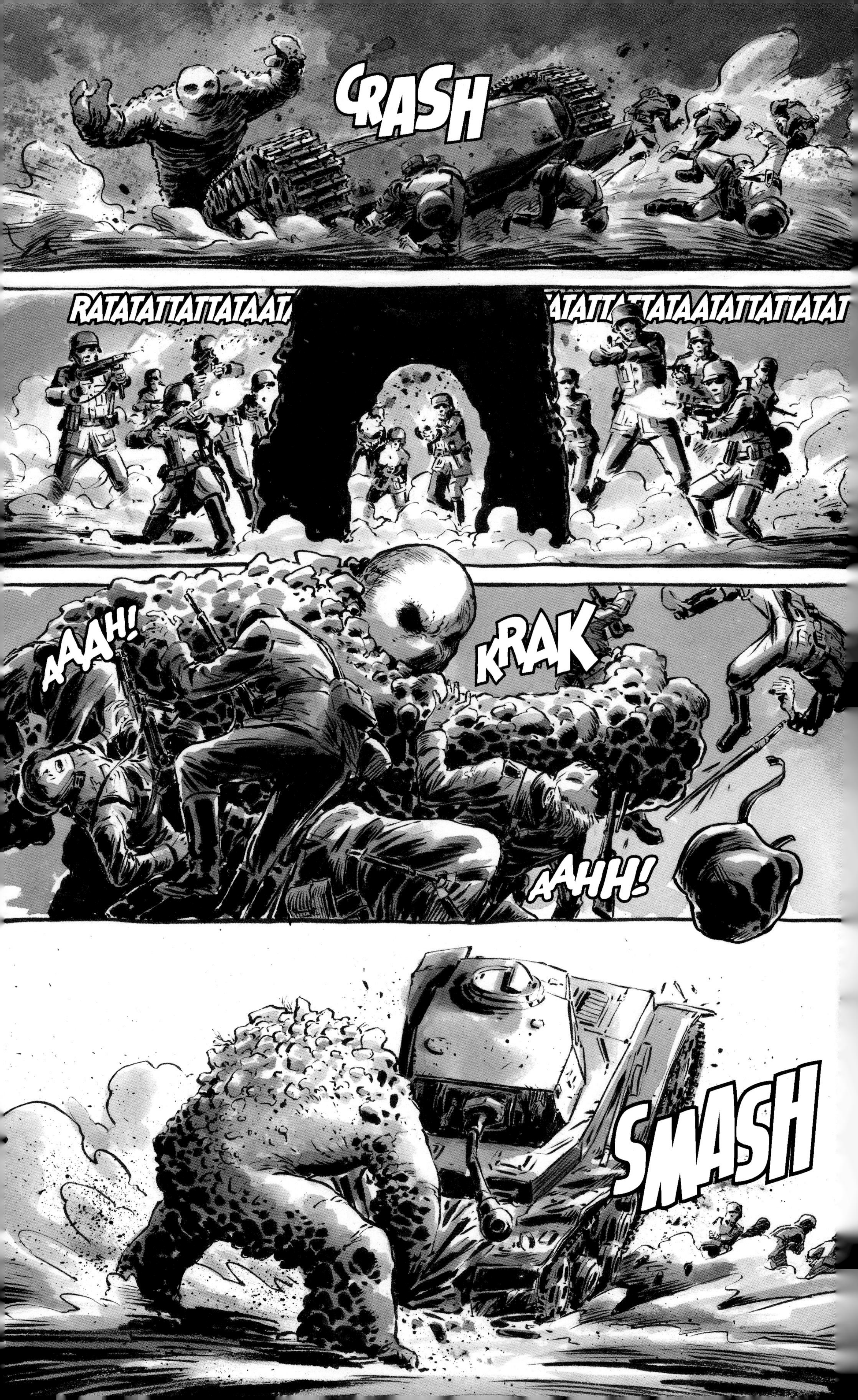
CRASH
RATATATTATTATAAT
ATATTATATAATATTATTATAT
AAAH!
KRAK
AAHH!
SMASH

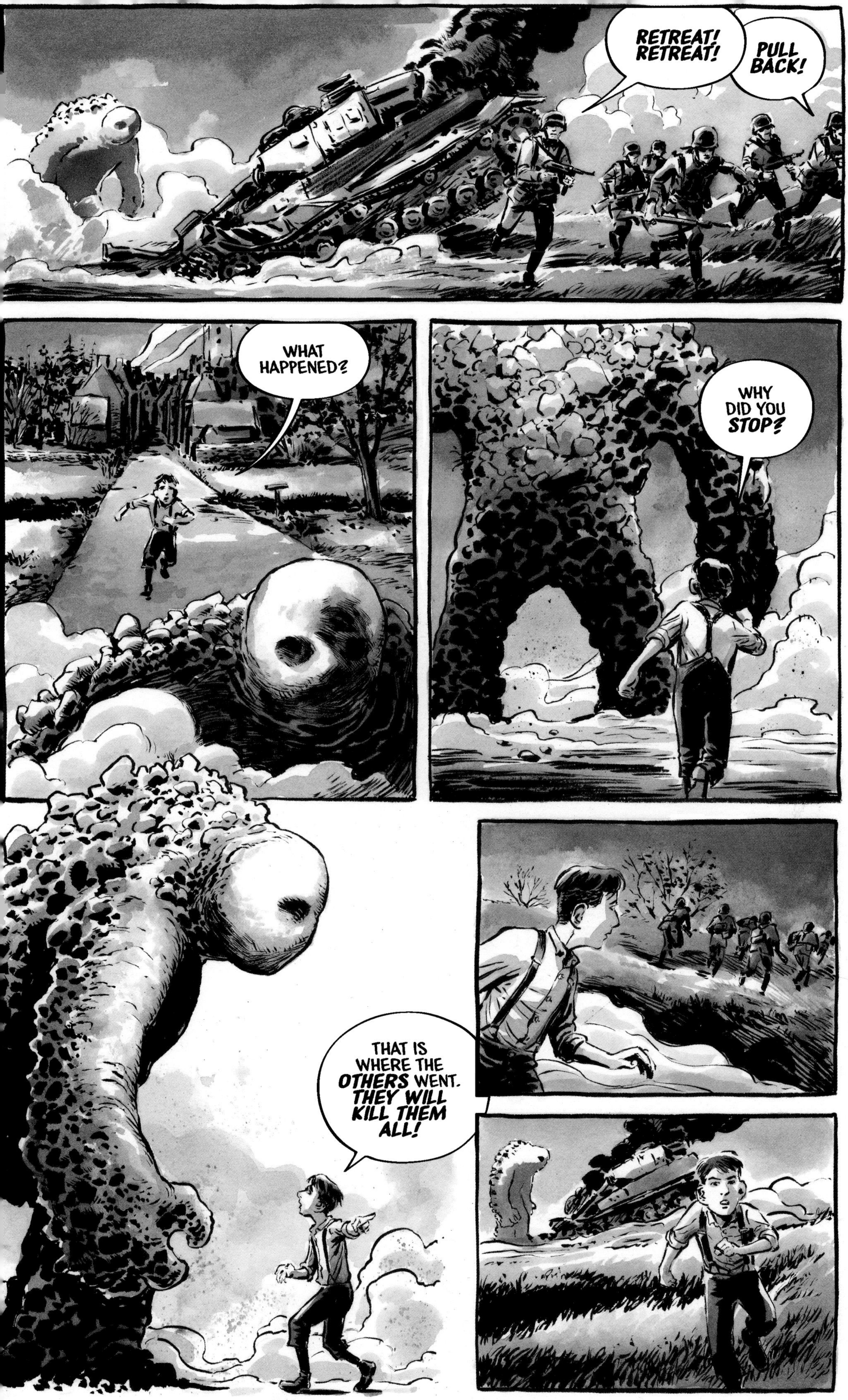
RETREAT! RETREAT!
PULL BACK!
WHAT HAPPENED?
WHY DID YOU STOP?
THAT IS WHERE THE OTHERS WENT. THEY WILL KILL THEM ALL!

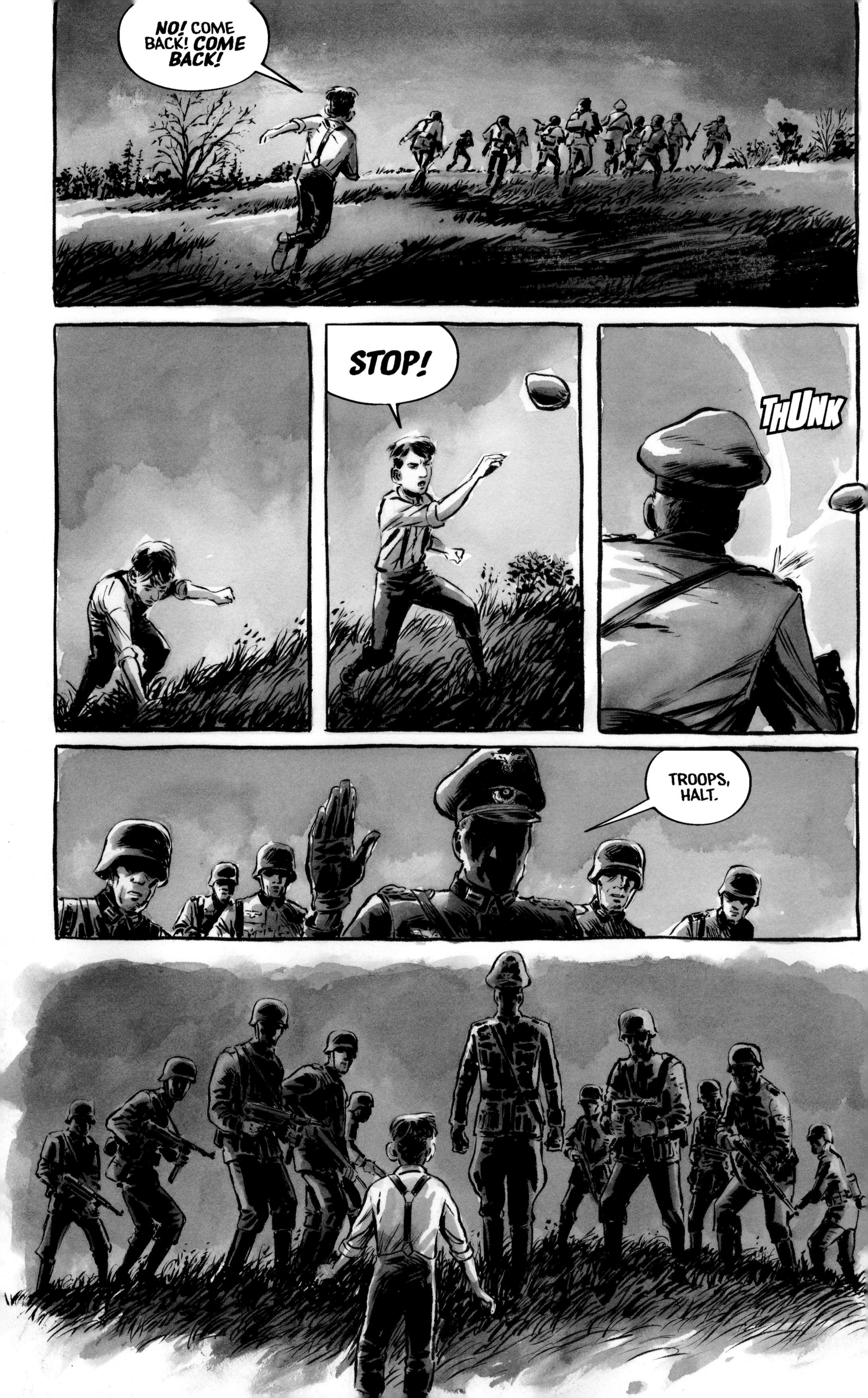
NO! COME BACK! COME BACK!
STOP!
THUNK
TROOPS, HALT.

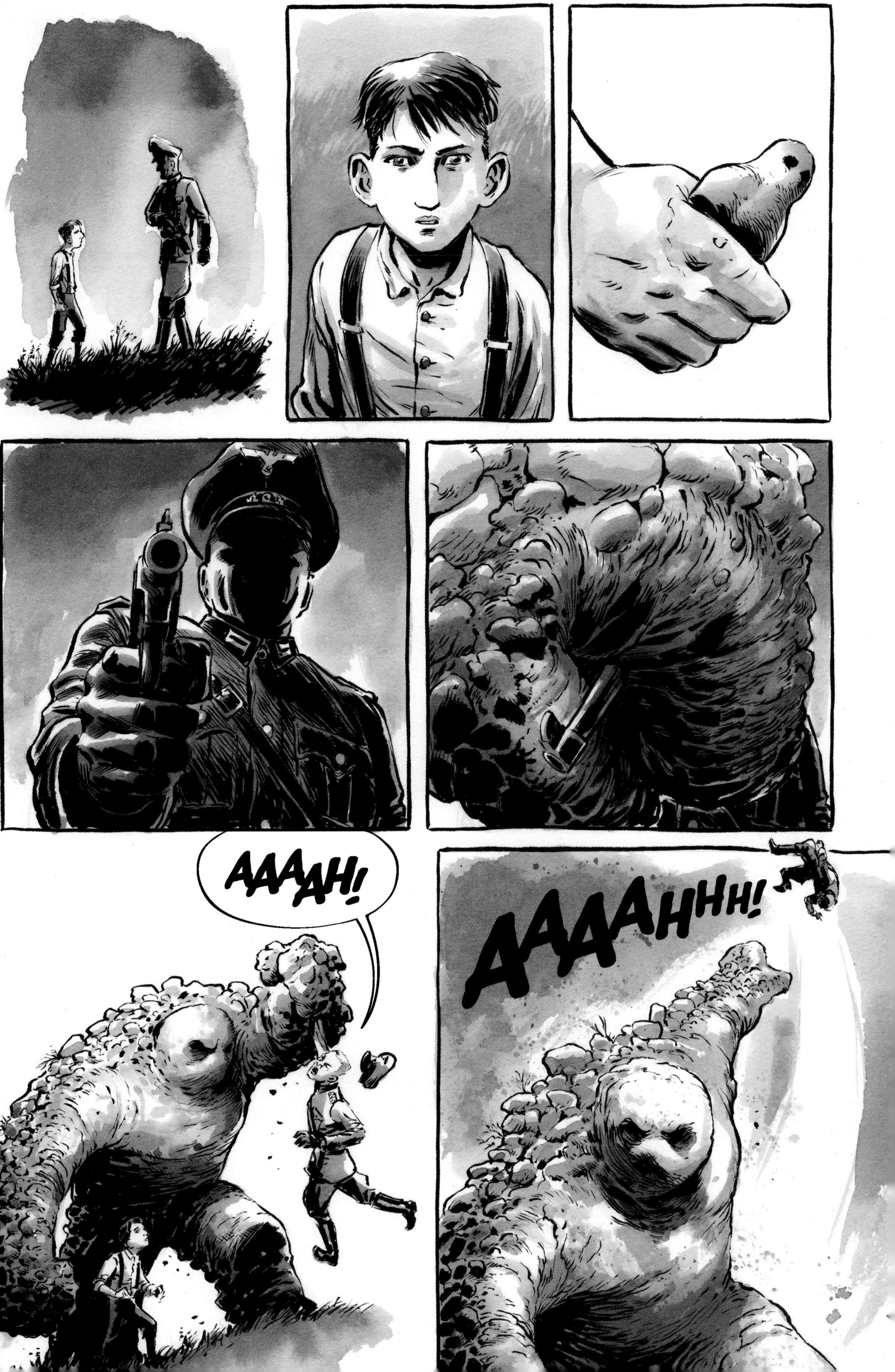
AAAAH!
AAAAHHH!

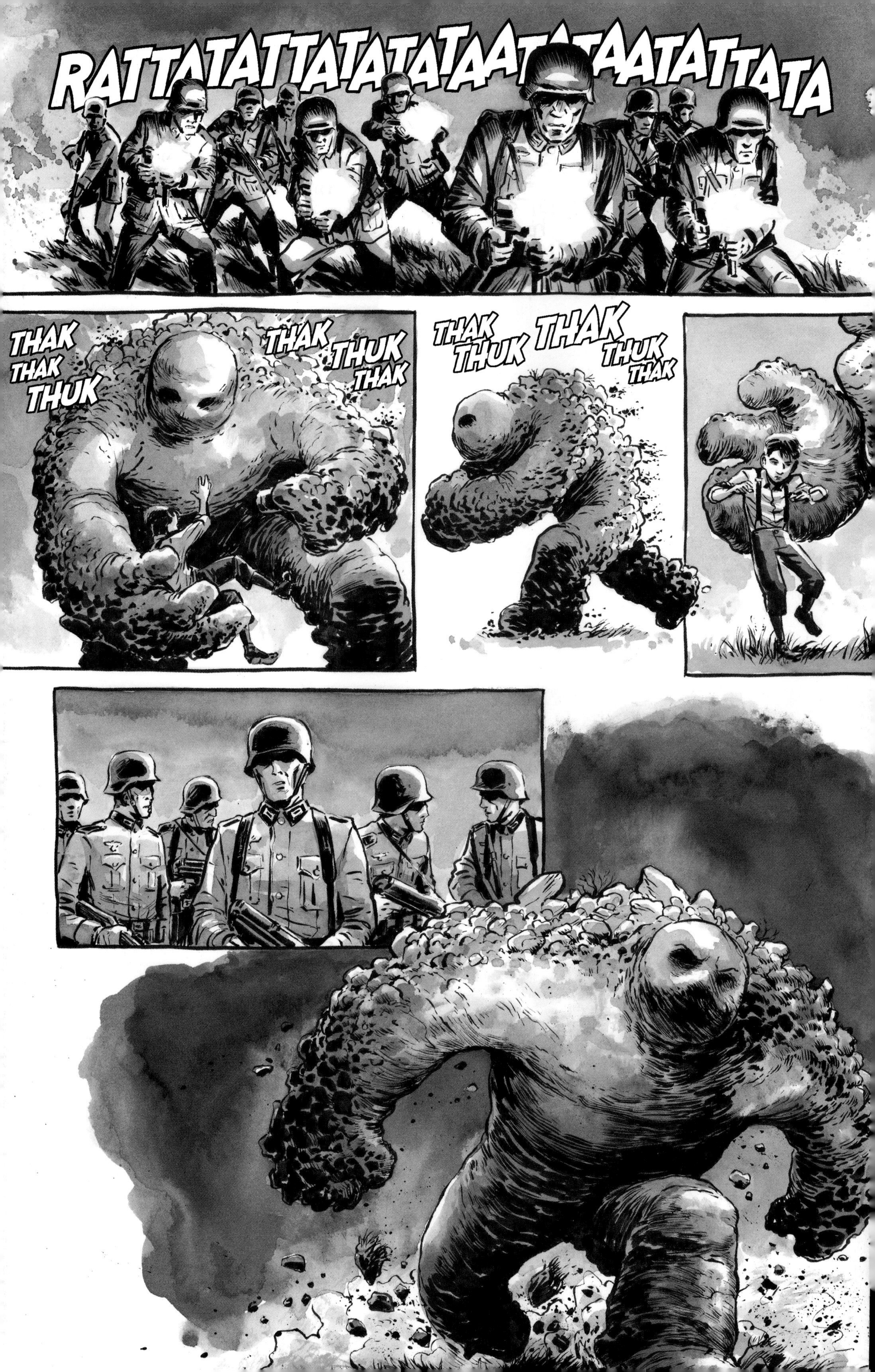
RATTATATTATATATAATATAATATTATA
THAK
THAK
THUK
THAK
THUK
THAK
THAK
THUK
THAK
THUK
THAK

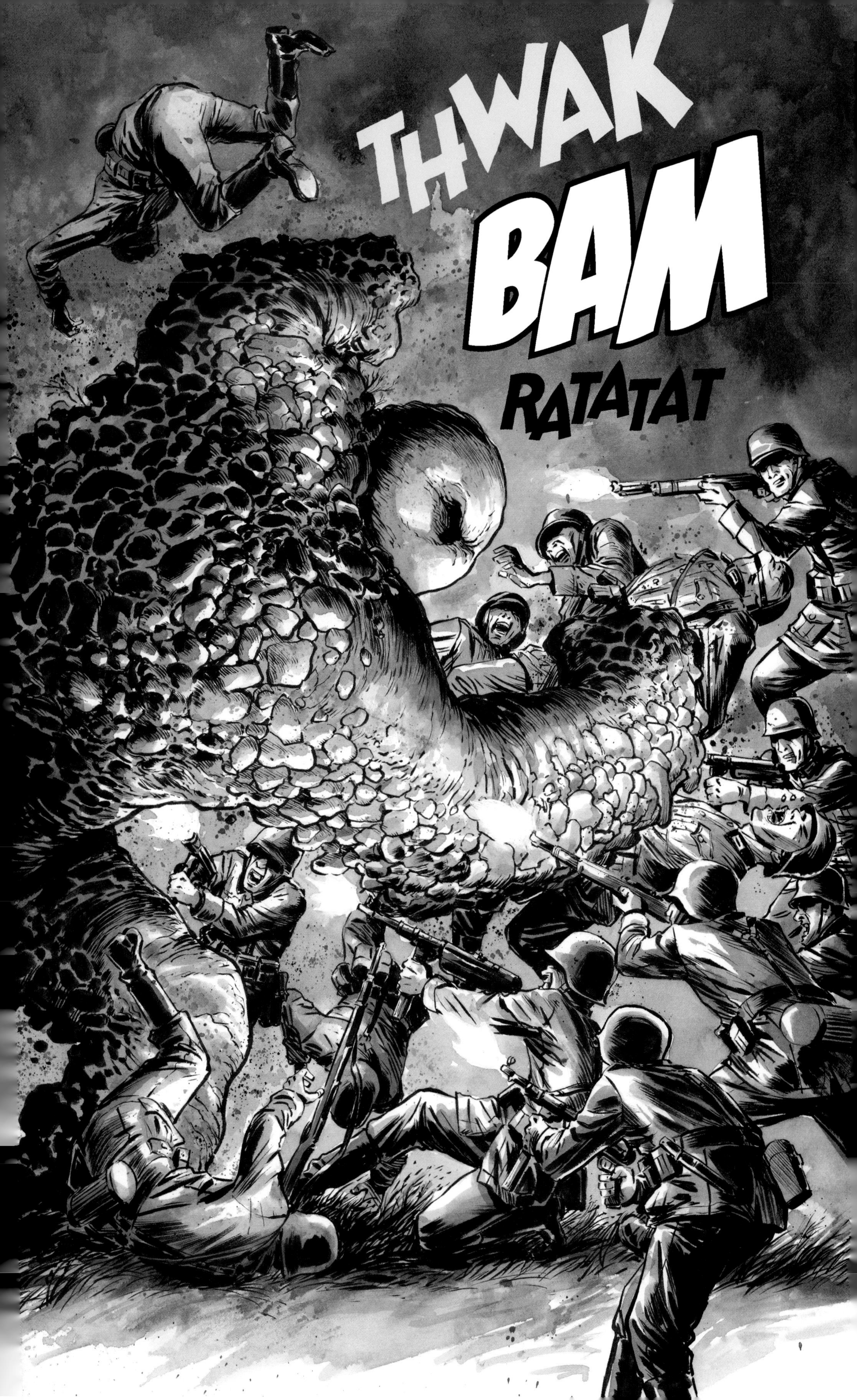
THWAK
BAM
RATATAT

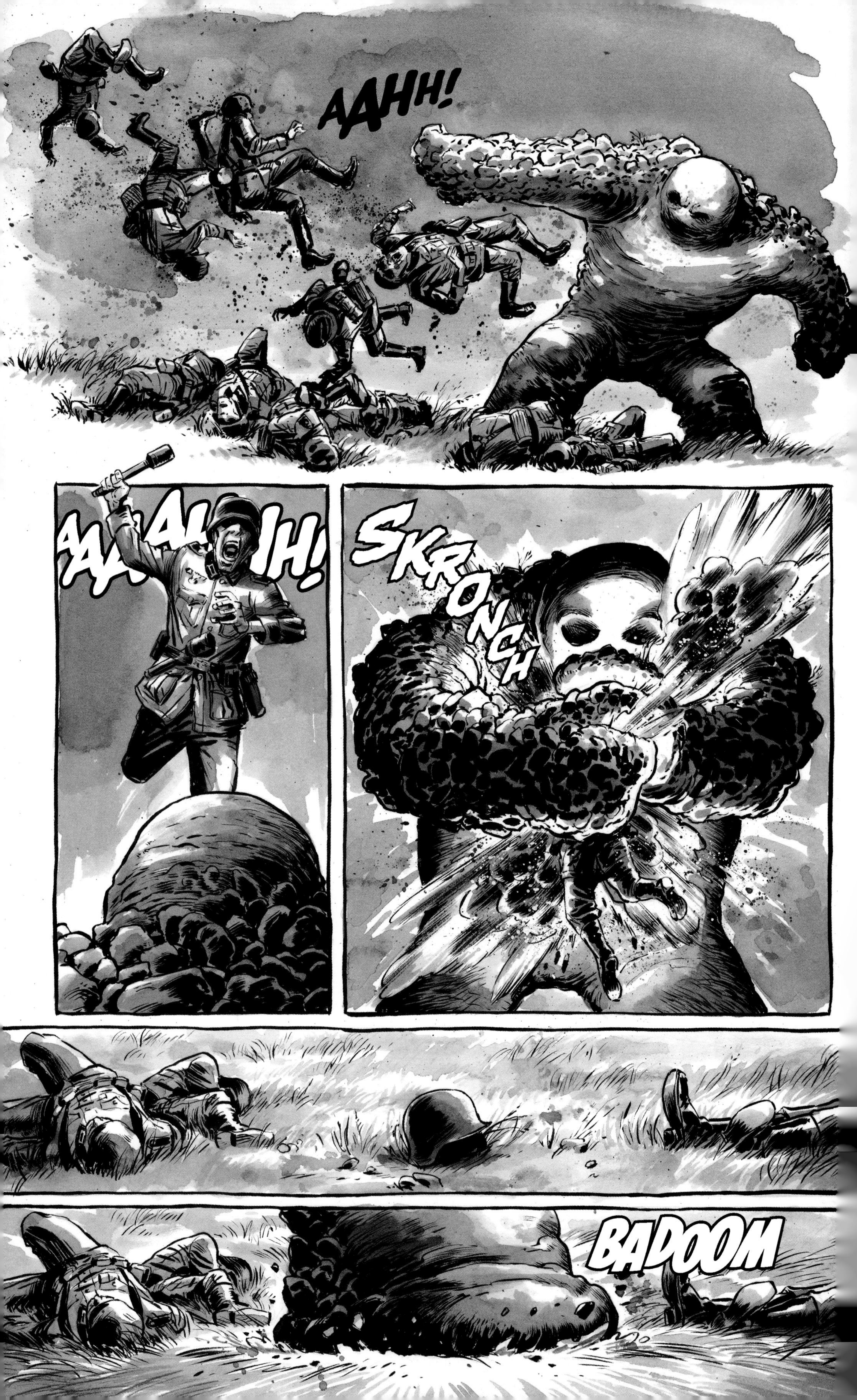
AAHH!
AAAAAHH!
SKRONCH
BADOOM

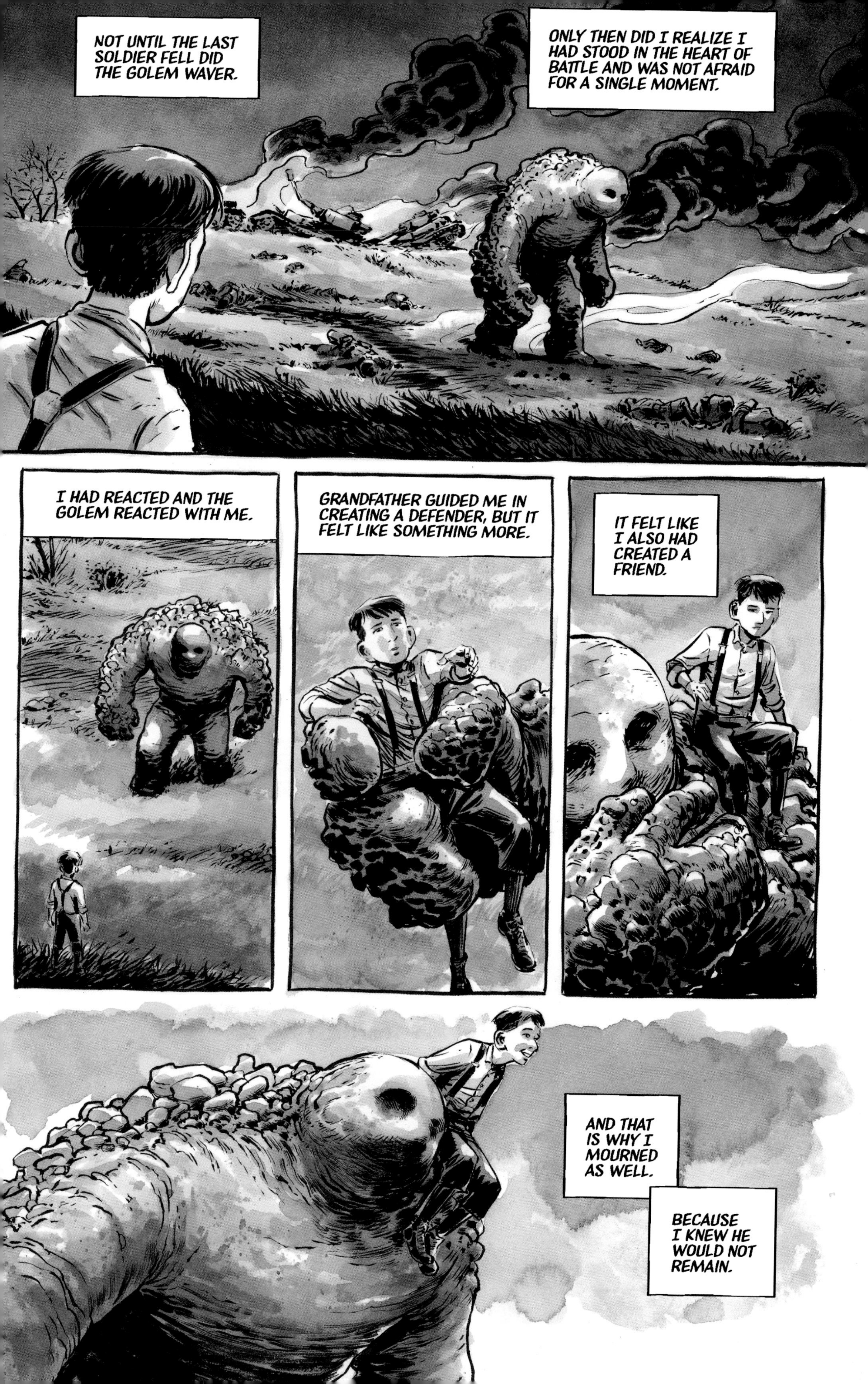
NOT UNTIL THE LAST SOLDIER FELL DID THE GOLEM WAVER.
ONLY THEN DID I REALIZE I HAD STOOD IN THE HEART OF BATTLE AND WAS NOT AFRAID FOR A SINGLE MOMENT.
I HAD REACTED AND THE GOLEM REACTED WITH ME.
GRANDFATHER GUIDED ME IN CREATING A DEFENDER, BUT IT FELT LIKE SOMETHING MORE.
IT FELT LIKE I ALSO HAD CREATED A FRIEND.
AND THAT IS WHY I MOURNED AS WELL.
BECAUSE I KNEW HE WOULD NOT REMAIN.

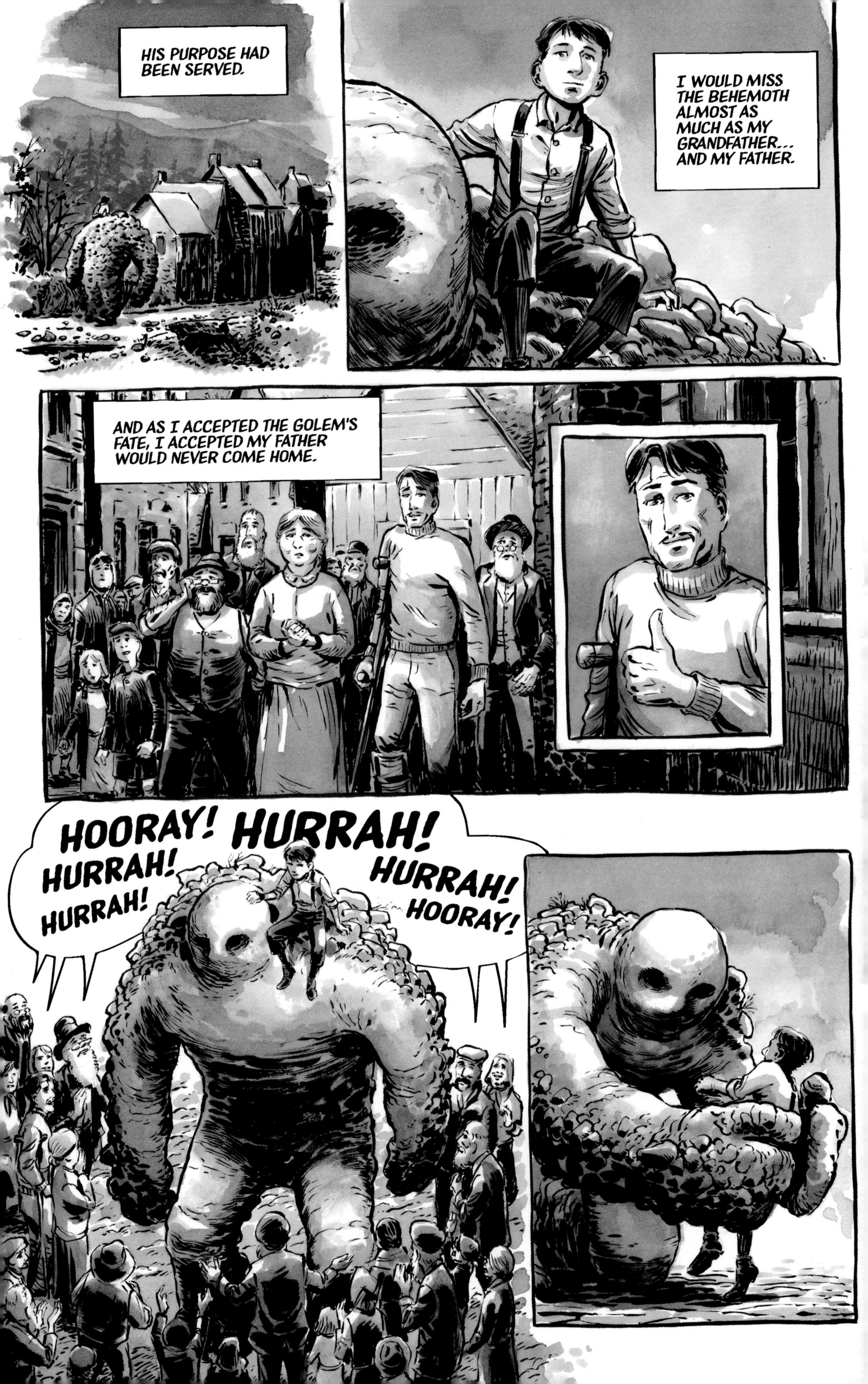
HIS PURPOSE HAD BEEN SERVED.
I WOULD MISS THE BEHEMOTH ALMOST AS MUCH AS MY GRANDFATHER... AND MY FATHER.
AND AS I ACCEPTED THE GOLEM'S FATE, I ACCEPTED MY FATHER WOULD NEVER COME HOME.
HOORAY! HURRAH! HURRAH! HURRAH! HURRAH! HOORAY!

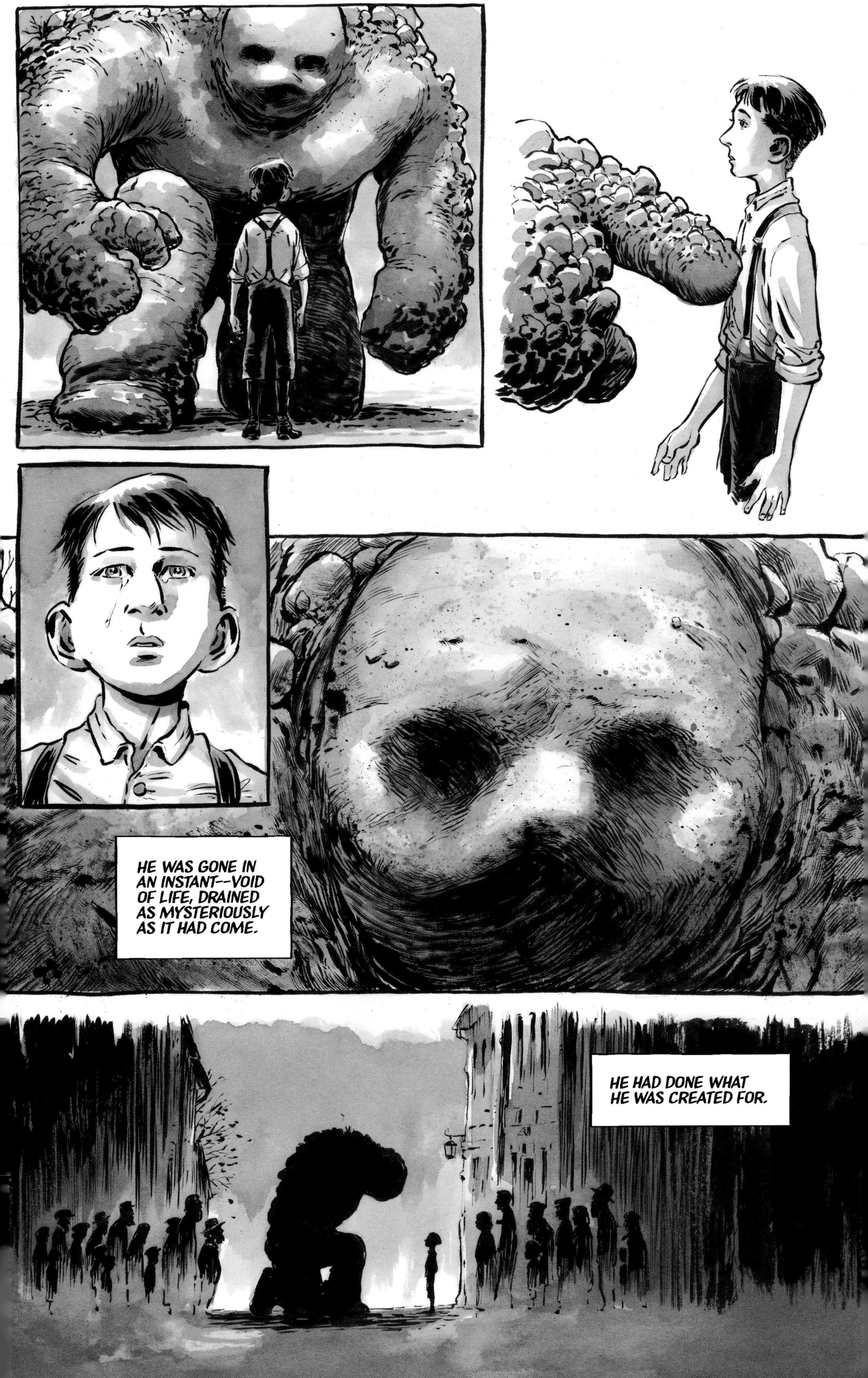
HE WAS GONE IN AN INSTANT--VOID OF LIFE, DRAINED AS MYSTERIOUSLY AS IT HAD COME.
HE HAD DONE WHAT HE WAS CREATED FOR.

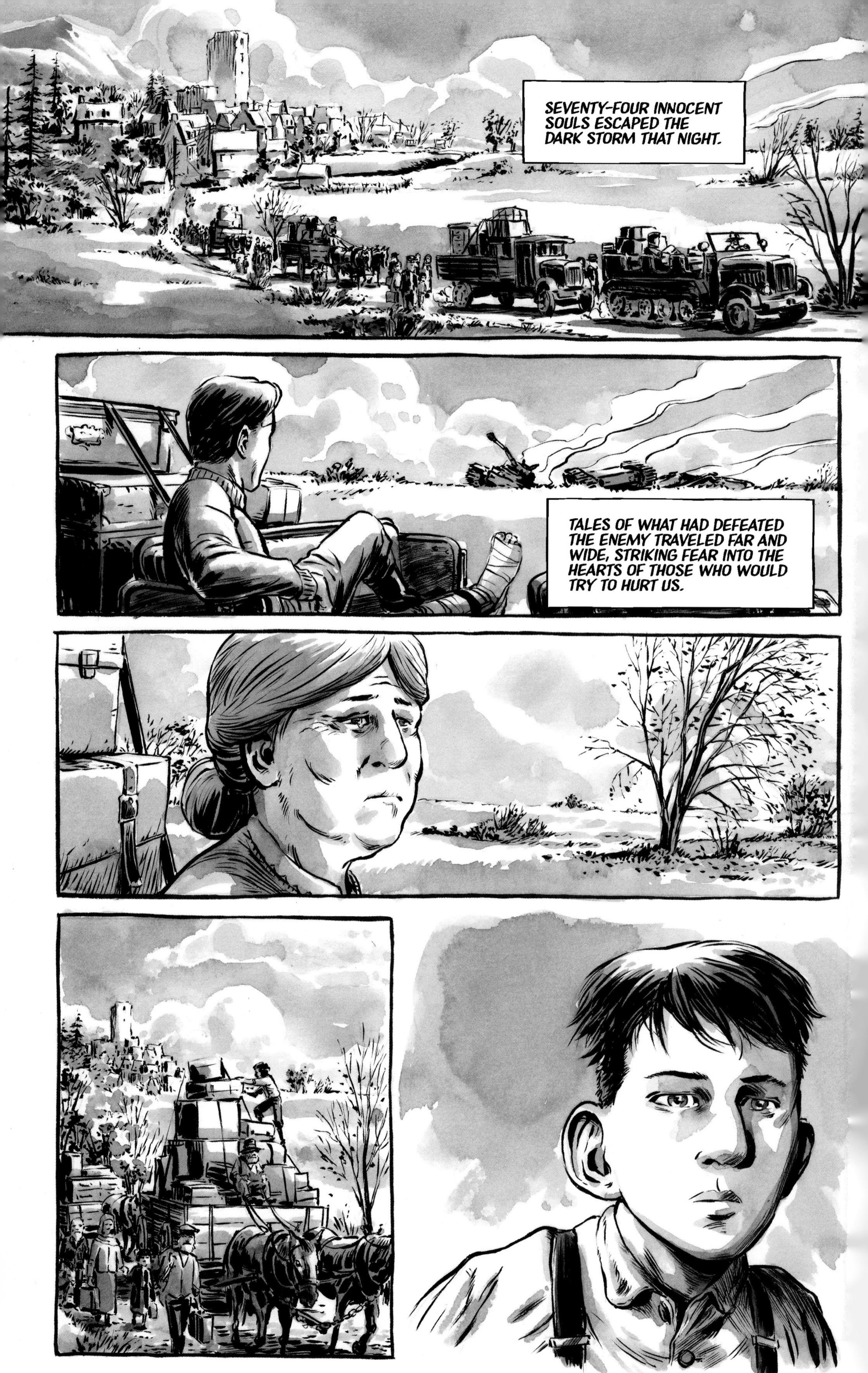
SEVENTY-FOUR INNOCENT SOULS ESCAPED THE DARK STORM THAT NIGHT.
TALES OF WHAT HAD DEFEATED THE ENEMY TRAVELED FAR AND WIDE, STRIKING FEAR INTO THE HEARTS OF THOSE WHO WOULD TRY TO HURT US.

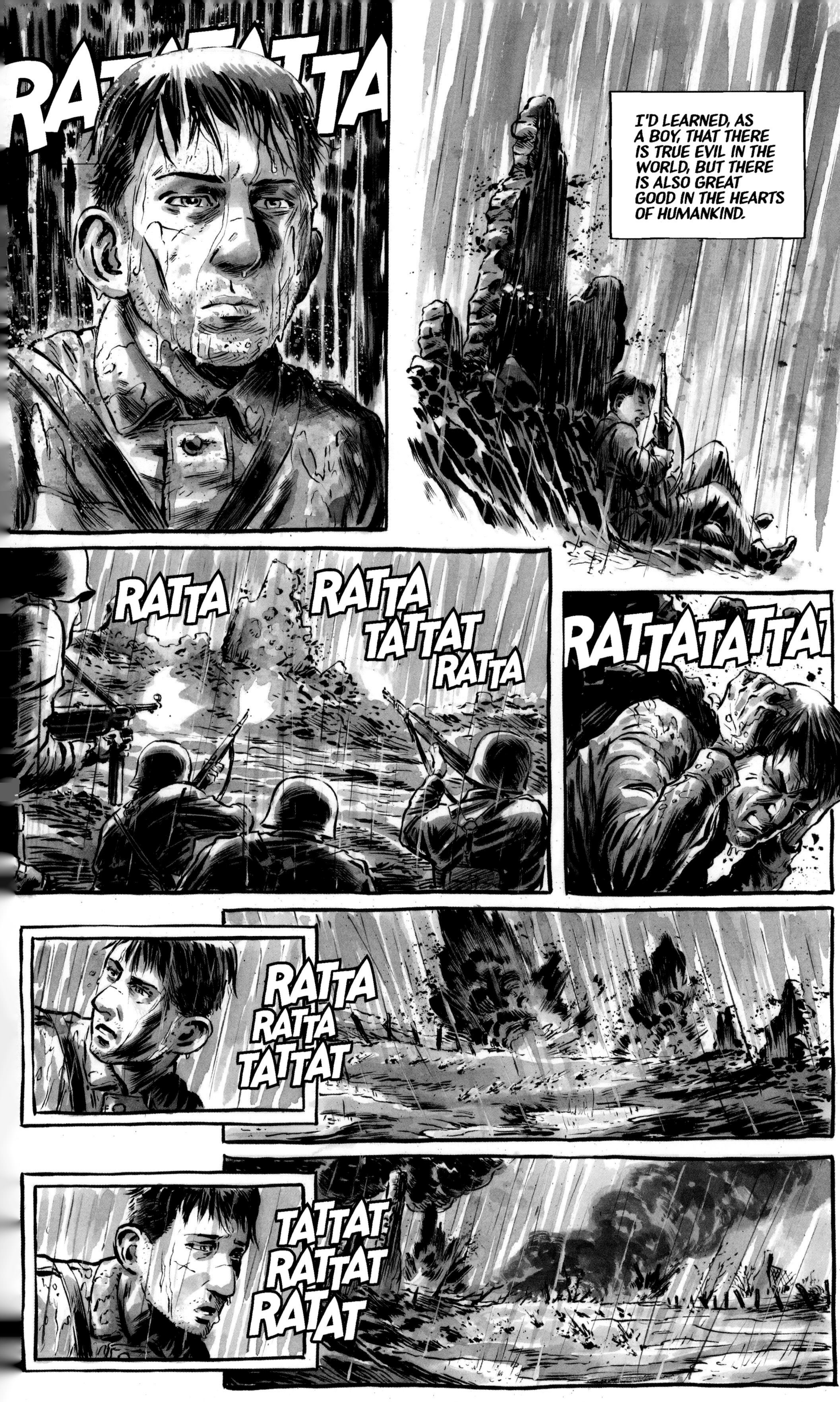
RATTATATTA
I'D LEARNED, AS A BOY, THAT THERE IS TRUE EVIL IN THE WORLD, BUT THERE IS ALSO GREAT GOOD IN THE HEARTS OF HUMANKIND.
RATTA
RATTA TATTAT RATTA
RATTATATTAT
RATTA RATTA TATTAT
TATTAT RATTAT RATAT

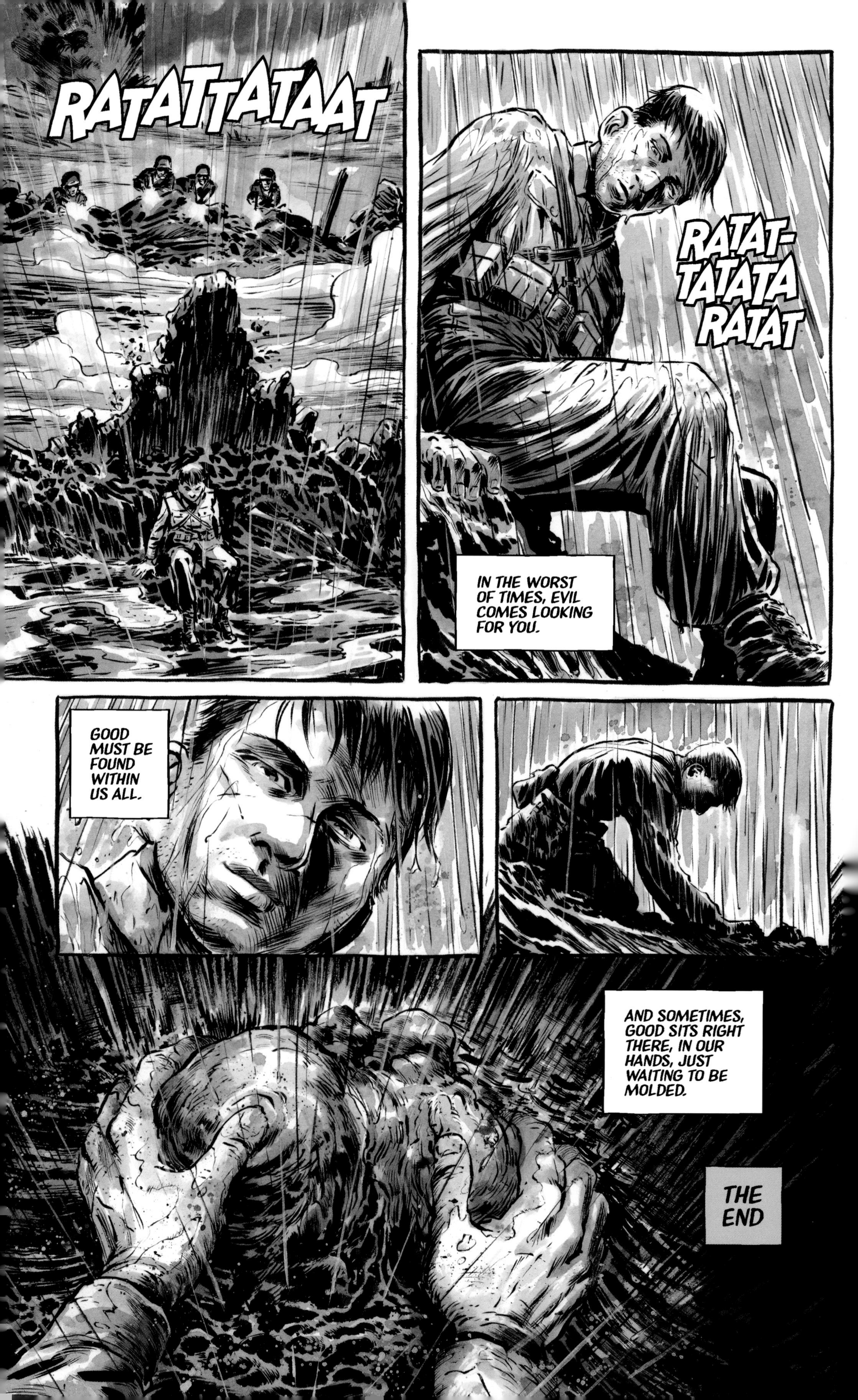
RATATTATAAT
RATAT-TATATA RATAT
IN THE WORST OF TIMES, EVIL COMES LOOKING FOR YOU.
GOOD MUST BE FOUND WITHIN US ALL.
AND SOMETIMES, GOOD SITS RIGHT THERE, IN OUR HANDS, JUST WAITING TO BE MOLDED.
THE END

SKETCHBOOK

Notes by Dave Wachter

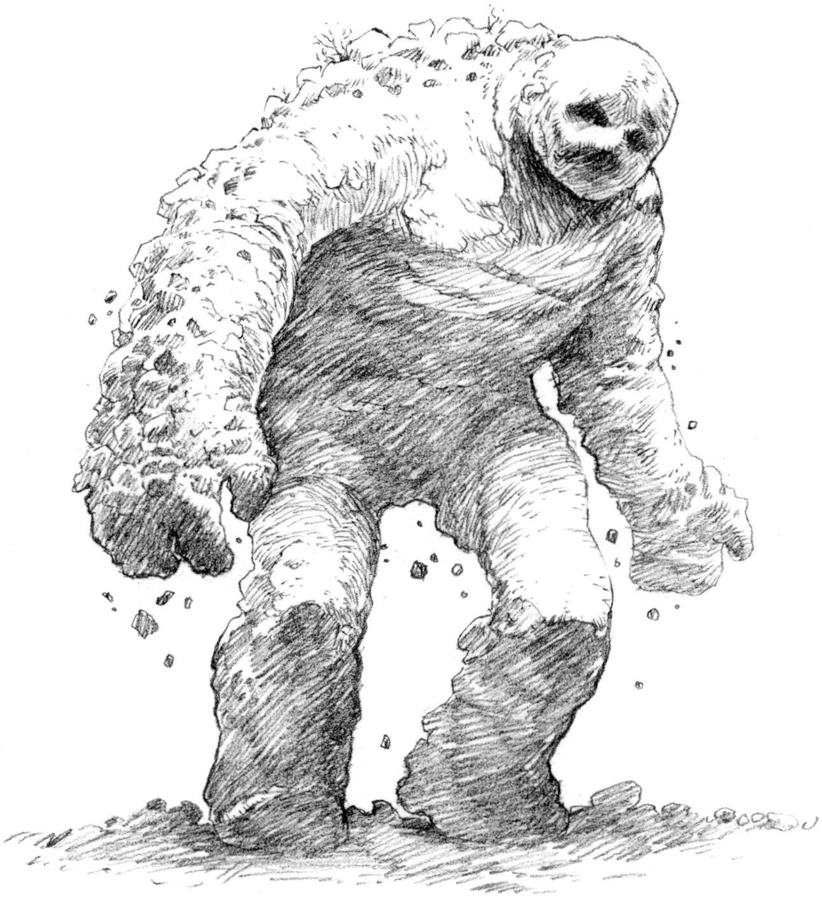

The golem was not crafted by an artisan. It was quickly and haphazardly pieced together by the villagers, with little plan or forethought. Thus, it's a very rough and lopsided design. As the golem stood to life, it dragged clumps of the ground with it. So while its front may be uneven, its back is a muddle of stone and mud, with the occasional plant root. Overall, this leads to bad posture.

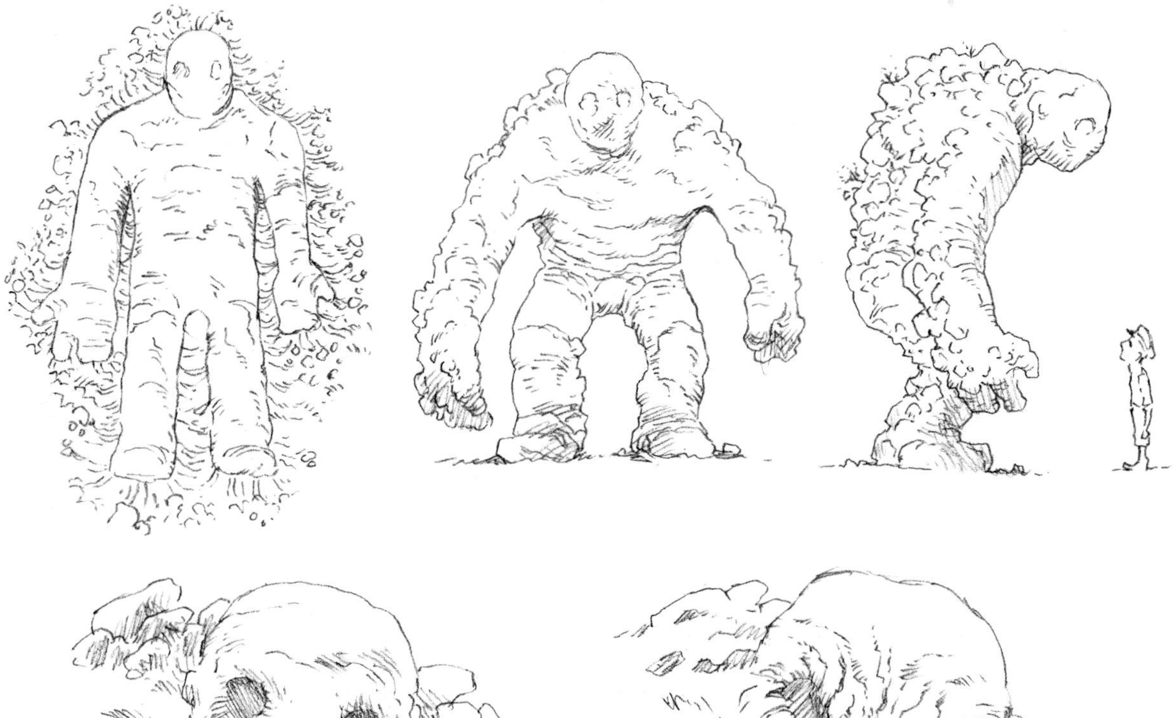

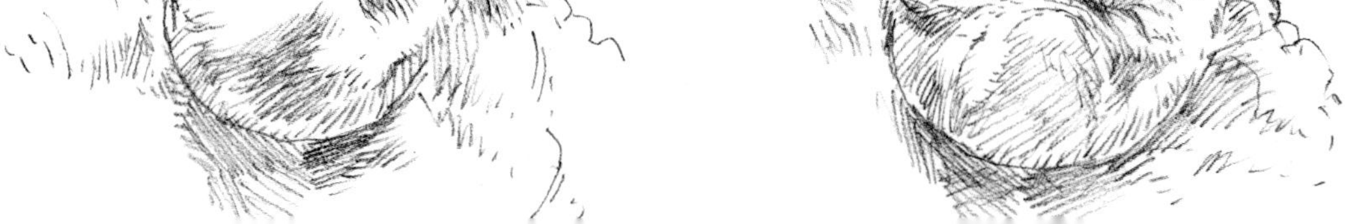

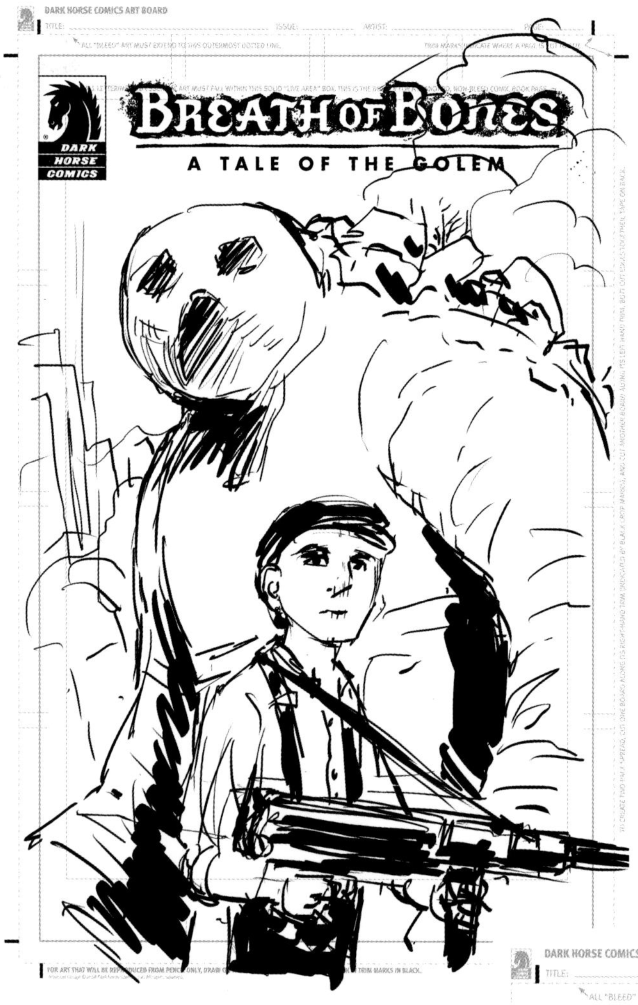
DARK HORSE COMICS ART BOARD
DARK HORSE COMICS
BREATH OF BONES
A TALE OF THE GOLEM

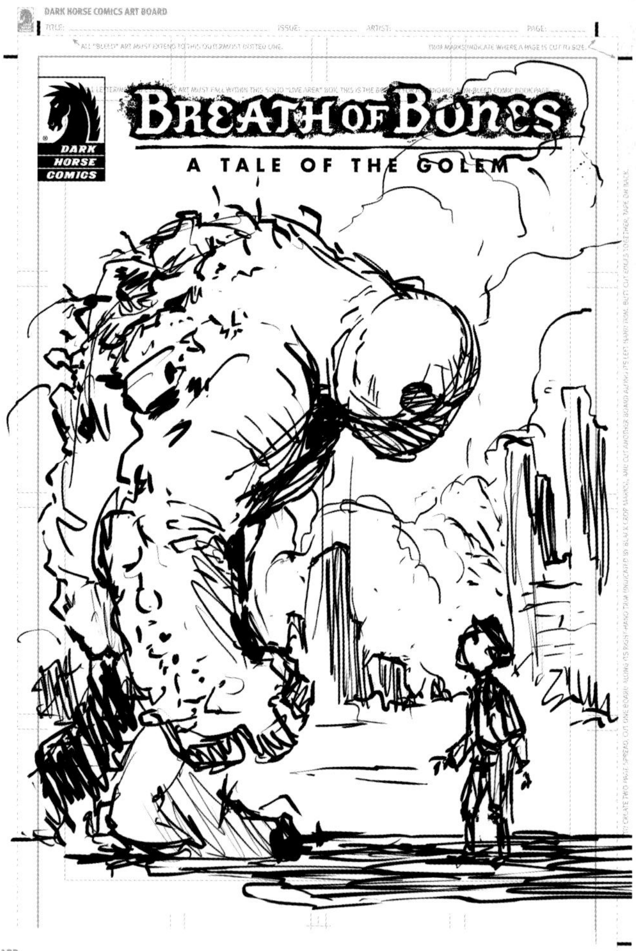
DARK HORSE COMICS ART BOARD
DARK HORSE COMICS
BREATH OF BONES
A TALE OF THE GOLEM

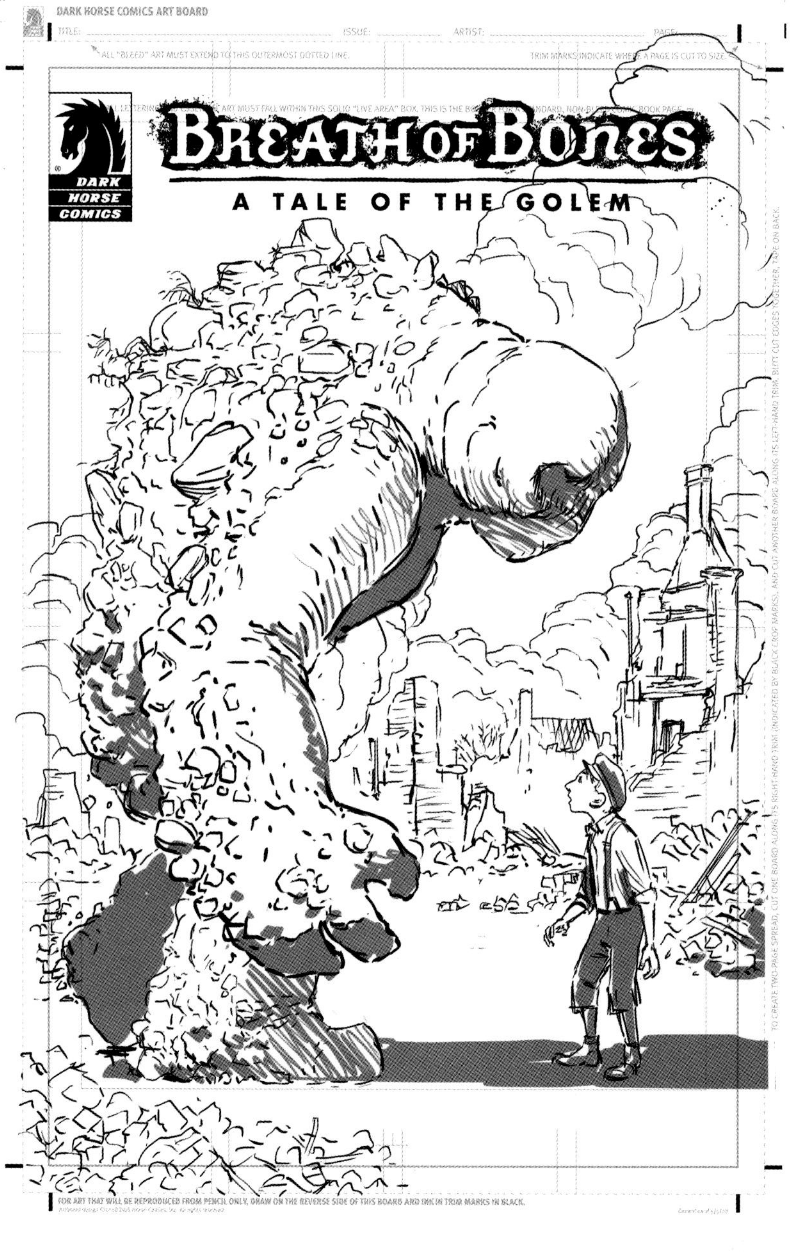
DARK HORSE COMICS ART BOARD
DARK HORSE COMICS
BREATH OF BONES
A TALE OF THE GOLEM
FOR ART THAT WILL BE REPRODUCED FROM PENCIL ONLY, DRAW ON THE REVERSE SIDE OF THIS BOARD AND INK IN TRIM MARKS IN BLACK.

Creating just the right cover design is a tough job for me. After all, I have to sum up the entire story in a single image that will also catch a prospective reader's attention. And often it has to be done without the benefit of the finished script. Above left you see an early design, with Noah holding a machine gun—which, after reading the story, we all can see is clearly out of place. And it's a boring design. There were plenty more where that came from.

The cover for issue #3 (and now the collected edition), right, is my favorite. I love drawing action-packed scenes, but it's the quiet moments that really pluck the ol' heartstrings. This design was originally created as an option for issue #2, but I'm glad we held off for the finale. It's so rare when a work truly encompasses all the ideas I wanted to express. And I didn't mess it up with the watercolors, so I was lucky.

BREATH OF BONES

A TALE OF THE GOLEM

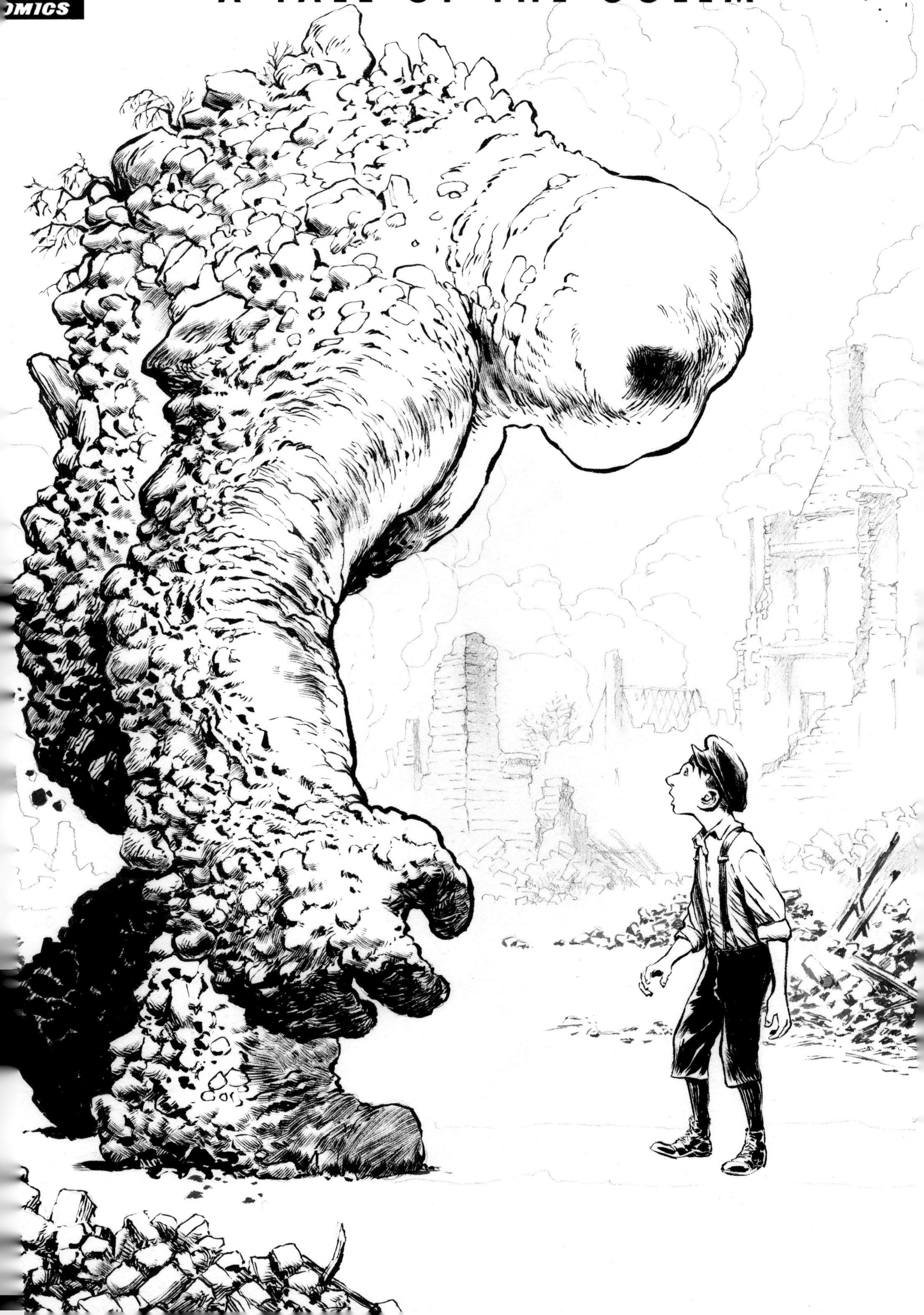

ALSO BY STEVE NILES

**CRIMINAL MACABRE:
THE EYES OF FRANKENSTEIN**
Steve Niles and Christopher Mitten
ISBN 978-1-61655-303-6 | $17.99

**CRIMINAL MACABRE OMNIBUS
VOLUME 1**
Steve Niles, Kelley Jones, and Ben Templesmith
ISBN 978-1-59582-746-3 | $24.99

VOLUME 2
Steve Niles, Kyle Hotz, Nick Stakal, and Casey Jones
ISBN 978-1-59582-747-0 | $24.99

**CRIMINAL MACABRE:
NO PEACE FOR DEAD MEN**
Steve Niles and Christopher Mitten
ISBN 978-1-61655-137-7 | $17.99

**CRIMINAL MACABRE:
THE IRON SPIRIT**
Steve Niles and Scott Morse
ISBN 978-1-59582-975-7 | $19.99

**CRIMINAL MACABRE:
FINAL NIGHT—THE 30 DAYS OF
NIGHT CROSSOVER**
Steve Niles and Christopher Mitten
ISBN 978-1-61655-142-1 | $17.99

**CRIMINAL MACABRE:
THE CAL MCDONALD CASEBOOK
VOLUME 1**
Steve Niles, Kelley Jones, Ben Templesmith, and Casey Jones
ISBN 978-1-61655-022-6 | $34.99

FREAKS OF THE HEARTLAND
Steve Niles and Greg Ruth
ISBN 978-1-59307-029-8 | $17.95

CITY OF OTHERS
Steve Niles and Bernie Wrightson
ISBN 978-1-59307-893-5 | $14.99

AVAILABLE AT YOUR LOCAL COMICS SHOP OR BOOKSTORE! • To find a comics shop in your area, call 1-888-266-4226.
For more information or to order direct visit DarkHorse.com or call 1-800-862-0052 Mon.–Fri. 9 AM to 5 PM Pacific Time. Prices and availability subject to change without notice.

DARK HORSE BOOKS
DarkHorse.com
drawing on your nightmares™

Criminal Macabre™ © Steve Niles. Text of Freaks of the Heartland™ © Steve Niles. Illustrations © Greg Ruth. City of Others © 2006, 2008 Steve Niles and Bernie Wrightson. All rights reserved. D